THE CHALLENGING ROAD TO SUCCESS

A Guided Road Map to Quality Mental, Physical, and Spiritual Habits for Your Journey to Success

DAVID L. ANGERON, PHD.

Copyright © 2025 David Angeron.

All rights reserved

Published by:

John Melvin Publishing, LLC

www.johnmelvinpublishing.com

ISBN: 978-1-7351627-5-1 Paperback

Images by Canva Pro

No part of this work may be reproduced or transmitted in any form or by any means, electronic, manual, photocopying, recording, or by any information storage and retrieval system, without prior written permission of the publisher.

Printed in the United States of America

Table of Contents

About the Author 1

Introduction 5

Foreword 9

Chapter 1: Redefining Success 19

Chapter 2: Overcoming Fear 39

Chapter 3: Mastering Stress Management 49

Chapter 4: Resilience 67

Chapter 5: Motivation 89

Chapter 6: Confidence 99

Chapter 7: Consistency: The Cornerstone of Excellence 109

Chapter 8: Meditation and Mindfulness - Unlocking Your Mental Potential 119

Chapter 9: Work Ethic – The Cornerstone for Success 137

Chapter 10: Setting SMARTER Goals: Your Path to Excellence 153

Chapter 11: Who Am I? Recognizing Personality Types 167

Chapter 12: Forging Mental and Physical Toughness 183

Chapter 13: Living in the Present - Carpe Diem 195

Chapter 14: What It Really Takes to Excel 205

Chapter 15: 30-Day Mind and Body Challenge: Unlock Your Full Potential 217

A Heartfelt Thank You 263

About the Author

www.davidangeron.com

David Angeron is a certified sport psychology coach and stress management expert who empowers athletes, performers, and business professionals to excel in sports, business, and life. With over two decades of experience coaching at various levels, from youth to professional athletes, Angeron has earned a reputation as an exceptional motivator and "players' coach." His expertise lies in unlocking human potential by applying lessons learned from sports and life experiences.

Angeron's journey into sport psychology began during his own multifaceted athletic career. Competing in baseball, football, soccer, basketball, and tennis throughout his youth, he faced numerous mental and emotional challenges. These experiences, coupled with being labeled as an undersized athlete, ignited his passion for understanding the psychological aspects of performance.

Defying expectations, Angeron went on to become a two-sport collegiate athlete in baseball and football. He attributes much of his success to his relentless focus on developing his mental game. This unique blend of personal experience and professional coaching has shaped his approach to sport psychology, allowing him to connect with and inspire athletes across various disciplines.

As the founder of Mental Master Training, LLC, Angeron specializes in comprehensive mental and physical performance training for athletes and performers. Additionally, he serves as the national recruiting coordinator for MyTime Sports, LLC, leveraging his extensive network built through years as a professional baseball scout to help aspiring athletes advance to collegiate and professional levels.

In 2022, Angeron and his wife Jean expanded their impact by founding John Melvin University, a private Christian institution specializing in Business, Sports Science, and Religious Studies. The university currently operates campuses in Crowley, LA, Pensacola, FL, and Winter Park, FL, furthering their commitment to education and personal development.

David currently resides in Pensacola, FL, with his wife, Jean Melvin Angeron. Together, they are proud parents to four children: Drake, Drew, Madeleine, and Reese. Through his work and personal life, Angeron continues to demonstrate the power of mental resilience and the importance of nurturing both mind and body in the pursuit of excellence.

About the Author

The Challenging Road to Success

INTRODUCTION

Welcome to your comprehensive guide for mental training and stress management, designed to propel you towards success. This book draws from years of expertise as a certified sport psychology coach, stress management specialist, former professional baseball general manager, ex-college athlete, motivational speaker, and lifelong baseball coach. The strategies and insights shared here are the culmination of extensive research and real-world experience.

Success is a deeply personal concept, one that often evolves as we grow and mature. In my youth, success meant autograph sessions after games, championship victories, luxurious homes, and high-end cars. By 26, I was living my dream as a professional baseball coach, enjoying VIP treatment, residing in a beachfront penthouse, and celebrating league championships. For a brief moment, I felt I had reached the pinnacle of success.

However, this feeling was short-lived. I soon became what I call a "Victim of Success." Depression set in, my marriage crumbled, and I lost my sense of purpose. The material possessions that once seemed so important now felt hollow. I left professional baseball to be closer to my children, realizing I had missed crucial years of their lives in pursuit of my career. My priorities had been severely misaligned, and I found myself stressed, depressed, and struggling to find meaning in life.

In a matter of years, I plummeted from the top of my game to rock bottom. Financial security gave way to near homelessness, and I found myself sleeping in my car at a truck stop. It was at this low point that I recognized my need for help. Through therapy and rekindling my relationship with God, I began to tap into mental toughness and resilience, marking the start of my true, challenging journey to success.

Today, after extensive research, continued education, and setting new goals, my perspective on success has transformed. I feel happier and healthier than ever before. This book offers you an insider's view of the arduous path to success, providing you with tools to craft your own roadmap. While many examples draw from my sports background, the strategies presented are universally applicable. Life itself is a competition, and adopting an athletic mindset can propel you towards your goals, regardless of your field.

The aim of this book extends beyond merely achieving success in sports, business, or personal life. It's about holistic growth - becoming a better person mentally, physically, and spiritually. As you embark on your journey to success, I encourage you to take notes and revisit chapters as needed. This book will serve as a valuable resource as you navigate obstacles in various aspects of life for years to come.

Introduction

Thank you for allowing me to be a part of your journey. I hope you find as much joy in reading this book as I found in writing it. Now, let's begin crafting your unique roadmap to success.

Enjoy the ride!

David L. Angeron, Ph.D.
Certified Sport Psychology Coach
Certified Stress Management Coach
www.davidangeron.com

The Challenging Road to Success

FOREWORD

"Success is predetermined by my faith, confidence, and belief in my products, services, and ideas. To be in harmony with my success, health, and happiness goals, I must act with love based upon free will and react with faith based upon God's will. To attract my Success, Health, and Happiness, I will eliminate fear of the future, worry over the past, and anxiety for the present." -Dr. James W. Parker, founder of Parker University.

The previous quote combines three of my favorite "Parker Principles" developed by world renowned chiropractor, Dr. James W. Parker. At some point, everyone who seeks a path to success must develop some key characteristics that will help guide them toward success. Ambition, desire, passion, confidence, determination, and persistence are just a few that are necessary to navigate through the resistance and adversity life will throw at you along your personal path to success. Most successful individuals will pick up or develop these characteristics with the aid of a parent, coach, or mentor starting at a young age. Others may develop them later in life. Regardless, everyone's path to success will look different. One thing is for certain, you will never reach or achieve success if you don't keep your motor running. Ambition and persistence in the face of adversity will propel you along your path.

I can recall being a young child watching my dad interact with my older brother in the front yard. I was three years old at the time and my brother was five. My dad was tossing him a plastic baseball and cheering and applauding with excitement as my brother swung the plastic bat and blasted the ball all the way across the front yard! I didn't quite understand the significance of what my brother was doing at the time, but I did know that I wanted and desired that same praise from my dad. I also wanted to swing that bat and smash that ball just like my brother could. My desire to compete and win started that easy, from the praise of a parent and natural want to compete for it with a sibling.

That passion only grew over the next few years as it was fueled by those glory-day sports stories my dad would tell my brother and me. My dad was our hero, and he had my brother and me hanging on every word. The sports tales may have gotten bigger and bigger each time he told them, but so did our dreams. We wanted those triumphs for ourselves! My dad must have picked up on the enthusiasm that my brother and I had for the desire to compete, because the stories and the pep-talks kept coming. He also kept tossing us those baseballs. But it didn't stop there. Baseballs turned to footballs and footballs turned to basketballs. As soon as we were old enough, he enrolled us in the local youth sporting league programs and even helped coach our teams.

Foreword

By playing organized sports, we developed a desire to compete, win, and succeed. We learned discipline, focus, and how to take instruction. We learned how to formulate goals and plans, and how to execute them. We learned how to identify and overcome obstacles. We developed confidence and self-worth. We were learning how to become winners in sports and in life. When we successfully completed a goal or task, we were taught how to thank God for that success. We were also taught how to pray and work hard for the things that we desired.

Those skillsets transcended into every aspect of life. In fact, for me, that same desire to compete and win carried over into the classroom. I quickly learned that the same praise that we received by making a great athletic play in a sporting event, was the same praise my mom would give when bringing home an 'A' on a test. And so, not only did I want to compete with my siblings and cousins with school grades, but I wanted to compete with every single classmate as well. At such a young age, with the aid of my will to compete and win, and with the proper guidance, I had already acquired the characteristics to achieve success in life. The big question was, "Were my developed characteristics strong enough to carry me through the adversity life was going to throw at me?"

I grew up in small 3-bedroom house that was supplemented by the government Section 8 housing subsidy program for low income families. For several years we had up to 8 people living in a small 3-bedroom home. We relied on Medicaid for healthcare and free lunches at school. We had to share our rooms and toys. We wore clothes that were passed down from older cousins or siblings. With so many people living in one house, keeping the house clean was a group effort. So naturally my mom delegated chores that we had to complete daily. Those chores taught us responsibility and accountability. I'm grateful for those early years of my life. I didn't know it at the time, but the characteristics I developed in those conditions were going to carry me through some of the toughest adversity yet to come.

I was about 8 years old when I received news that my dad was severely hurt on a job at work. A scaffold board malfunctioned that caused my dad to fall about 6-7 feet and land onto a piece of steel below. The steel pierced his back, punctured a lung, broke several ribs, and fractured a bone in his lumbar spine. Thankfully, his spinal cord was spared, but the injuries were severe. Due to the injuries and the pain, he developed severe depression and a dependency on opioids. He also began to drink heavily on top of the medications. We barely had any income coming in as a family, so we had to sacrifice even more than we did prior to his accident. Eventually my dad's dependency issues, his depression, and our family's financial struggles led to irreparable problems between my parents. I witnessed some ugly domestic disputes. Arguments would often turn physical, and my siblings and I would occasionally become collateral damage.

My parents eventually separated, and we could not afford to live in our home anymore. My mom, my siblings, and I were forced to move to another town into a run-down rent house. We couldn't afford cable, and half the time didn't have a home phone. Sometimes I would come home to find that the electricity and gas were cut off. Sometimes we were without a vehicle, so my brother and I relied on the bus and friends for transportation. After a few years, we couldn't afford to live at that place anymore. We had to move into a rent house about half the size. From there, we continued to bounce around every 6 months to a year from rent house to rent house. Eventually, we couldn't even afford to do that anymore. From that point, we started living with family members for weeks to months at a time. All of the moving around was becoming really hard for me to get to school and sporting events. So, by the time I was a 17-year-old senior in high school, I started living at my friends' houses just to get to school easier. Through the adversity, my drive for success only grew stronger. I maintained a 3.9 GPA throughout my four years of high school and graduated as a top-ten student. It remains one of the biggest accomplishments of my life.

Though I promised myself as a young child that I would strive to become a professional athlete, my mom taught me that academics would always be my safety net. And so, I always put academics first. I can recall leaving football or baseball games tired and sore, and immediately switching my mind frame to my studies. I never lost focus on what was important, no matter how poor my living conditions were. Still, my athletic talents did not go unnoticed. I was a first team Academic All-State award recipient in football and baseball and did get some college scholarship offers. I recall getting a couple of DII baseball and football offers that I turned down for an opportunity to play football at a local DI college. However, by the time I graduated high school and summer rolled around, nothing was going to plan. I didn't have a vehicle or a stable home. A few plans that I had made to move to prepare for school and football fell through. Instead of enrolling at the university and playing football, I sat out of college entirely for the first semester and went to work. I ended up enrolling in a local college the following semester so that I could commute with some friends 45 minutes to campus. I started a pre-med biology program and decided to give up on the athletic dream. After my first 2 years of college, I was finally able to afford my first vehicle. Over the next 3 years, with a lot of hard work, I completed my undergraduate studies.

Seeing my dad's recovery from his work injury with the aid of his chiropractic physician must have made a sub-conscious impression upon me that I carried with me all those years. It eventually prompted me to apply for the Chiropractic Physical Medicine program at Parker University in Dallas, Texas. I was thrilled when I was immediately accepted. I went on to Dallas, Texas where I completed the 4-year program in 3 ½ years and graduated in the top ten of my graduation class with honors. This was another major accomplishment in my life.

I have been in private practice for 10 years now. For the last 8 years I have had a practice where I focus on personal injury care including motor-vehicle collision injuries and work-related injuries.

Foreword

Perhaps witnessing my dad's injury and knowing the effects the injury had on him and my family sub-consciously drove me to this type of practice. I wanted to help people return to their normal lives because I know what the devastating effects of these injuries can be for the patients and their families. To date, I have treated thousands of personal injury patients, and I receive referrals from personal injury attorneys from all over the state of Louisiana. I have even been called on to testify in court in some of these injury cases as an expert witness in the field of Chiropractic. It's been a rewarding career to date to say the least. No matter how great these accomplishments may seem, my biggest accomplishment of my life is and will remain to be having a beautiful wife and daughter to go home to, Nicole and Sadie.

I guess you can say that the drive to succeed that was instilled within me as a child never faltered. The road was tough and unpredictable, but I remained persistent. My determination only grew with every bump in the road. David Angeron was one of those influential mentors and coaches that helped guide me along my road to success. David entered my life when I was around 13 years old while he was scouting one of my all-star baseball teams. I quickly received word that he was interested in me playing third base for him as he would be taking over as the head coach of our town's high school baseball team. David spotted my will and determination to win within hours. He had already begun to impact my life. I had never met a coach with a passion for baseball that was so immediately infectious. When I was in the presence of great mentors like David, my problems at home didn't exist. David proceeded to coach me in football and baseball over the next 4 years. He was aware of some of my struggles at home, so he even allowed me to cut his grass for money whenever needed, as he knew my mom struggled to pay for our required athletic gear. Even then he was mentoring me to develop my work-ethic. I am forever grateful for the way Coach David Angeron impacted my life.

David's book, "The Challenging Road to Success", is a 30-day roadmap that any inspiring athlete, or inspiring professional of any field, can read and utilize to help reach their personal success destination. David really hit a homerun with this guide. Starting with the first chapter he identifies the different types of stresses that individuals must identify and learn to manage if they want to successfully accomplish their goals. David goes on to teach techniques for overcoming fear while developing motivation, confidence, and work-ethic. These are some of the same characteristics that David helped me to shape and develop as an adolescent playing football and baseball. In one of my favorite chapters, David touches on developing and utilizing resiliency to overcome adversity. This chapter really touched my heart and summed up a large piece of my life story. David proceeds to break down personality types and how to identify your own so that you have one more tool in your toolbox that will help you navigate through your personal adversity on the way to success. Identifying your personality type may help you choose the appropriate courses of action when solving conflicts along your path. Physical and mental toughness are must-have characteristics required to succeed in any professional atmosphere. The fact that you are reading this

Foreword

book means that you already have the innate desire to succeed. Let David's guide fine-tune your game plan and shorten your path to success by helping you to effectively navigate through obstacles that are impeding your journey.

Wishing You Success,
Dr. Shane M. Chaisson
Chiropractic Physician
New Iberia, Louisiana

The Challenging Road to Success

Chapter 1

REDEFINING SUCCESS

What is True Success?

Marcus Aurelius, the great stoic philosopher, profoundly stated, "Success is to look upon all things in the world quietly and kindly; accept all things the way they are" (Book 5, P. 131-151). This powerful insight challenges us to reconsider our conventional notions of success and embrace a more enlightened perspective.

By adopting this mindset, we can shield ourselves from the allure of external validation - fame, fortune, and wealth. While these may seem enticing, true success lies in mastering our internal landscape. Remember, reason must be our guiding light when pride and conceit threaten to cloud our judgment. Humility is the antidote to pride, and it's through humility that we can fully appreciate and internalize our achievements.

Consider this: unless you pour your heart into your work, it becomes mere drudgery, destined for failure. The highest form of success is found in the spirit with which you approach your tasks. As the Bible reminds us, God doesn't say, "Well done, thou good and successful servant," but rather, "Well done, thou good and faithful servant" (Matthew 25:21, KJV). This powerful message implores us to redirect our focus, cultivate our appetite for meaningful work, and above all, remain faithful to our purpose.

Embrace this transformative truth: God commends the faithful, not merely the successful. Cultivate your appetite for purpose-driven work and unwavering faithfulness.

Why is it crucial to understand success in this light? Why must we redirect our appetites and unlearn our preconceptions? Because at the pinnacle of achievement, the risk of downfall is ever-present. By redefining success, we protect ourselves from becoming victims of our own accomplishments.

As a lifelong professional baseball coach, scout, and general manager, I've had the privilege of being a friend and mentor to many. My experience as a certified sport psychology coach and stress management expert has allowed me to guide countless athletes and business professionals towards improved performance, unlocked potential, and genuine happiness. In the chapters that follow, I'll share invaluable insights on setting smart, achievable goals, developing a robust work ethic, building resilience and confidence, and nurturing strong mental, emotional, and spiritual well-being - all essential components of a truly successful life.

But first, let's challenge ourselves. Epictetus, another great philosopher, warns us, "It is impossible for a person to begin to learn what he thinks he already knows" (Book 2, Ch.17, P. 247). So, let's open our minds and hearts as we explore: What is true success?

Redefining Success

Success [suhk-ses]
Noun
- The favorable or prosperous termination of attempts or endeavors; the accomplishment of one's goals.

- The attainment of wealth, position, honors, or the like.
- A performance or achievement that is marked by success, as by the attainment of honors.
- A person or thing that has had success, as measured by attainment of goals, wealth, etc.

But I challenge you: What does success truly mean to you? This powerful term carries different meanings for different individuals. While many equate success with wealth, this is a limited perspective. True success is a profound feeling of self-fulfillment derived from achieving personal and professional goals that align with your values and purpose.

Throughout my extensive personal and professional journey, I've distilled the essence of success into four fundamental pillars. These aren't just abstract concepts - they're the cornerstones of a truly fulfilled life that I'm excited to share with you.

The Four Pillars of Success:
1. Physical Success
2. Mental Success
3. Personal Success
4. Spiritual Success

Physical Success:

From the dawn of humanity, our species has thrived by adapting to diverse and challenging environments. The phrase "survival of the fittest" isn't just a cliché - it's a fundamental truth of our existence. Physical success isn't merely about looking good; it's about feeling vibrant and capable in any situation. It encompasses your biological health, your fitness level, and your ability to face life's challenges head-on.

Imagine reaching the pinnacle of your career, only to find yourself too exhausted or ill to enjoy it. That's not success - that's sacrifice. True physical success means having the energy and vitality to not just survive, but to thrive in the face of adversity. It's about embracing life's challenges as opportunities for growth, not obstacles to overcome.

Mental Success:

Your mind craves novelty and growth. It's not enough to simply exist - you need to evolve, to challenge yourself, to push beyond your comfort zone. Mental success isn't just about intelligence; it's about cultivating a positive mindset, building unshakeable self-respect, and finding inner peace.

Consider the great innovators of history - they didn't just accept the world as it was; they imagined how it could be better. That's the essence of mental success. It's about forging strong connections with mentors and thought leaders, constantly learning and adapting, and viewing every experience as an opportunity for growth. When you achieve mental success, you're not just surviving in the world - you're actively shaping it.

PERSONAL SUCCESS

Personal Success:

True personal success isn't measured by the size of your bank account - it's measured by the richness of your life experiences. It encompasses your career achievements, your economic stability, and crucially, the quality of your relationships and your impact on society.

Ask yourself: Are you inspiring others? Are people eager to follow your lead? Or are you burning out, chasing an elusive definition of success? Personal success means leaving a positive mark on the world, no matter how small. It's about making a difference, about ensuring that the world is somehow better because you were here. That's the kind of success that truly matters - the kind that leaves a lasting legacy.

Spiritual Success:

Spiritual success is the cornerstone of a truly fulfilled life. It's about understanding your place in the universe, finding your higher purpose, and living in alignment with your deepest values. It's not just about religious beliefs - it's about cultivating qualities like discipline, honesty, loyalty, and love.

Consider this profound question: "What good will it be for a man if he gains the whole world, yet forfeits his soul?" Spiritual success means choosing contentment over materialism, kindness over conflict, and generosity over greed. It's about leaving a spiritual heritage that inspires and uplifts others long after you're gone.

Embracing the Four Pillars of Success

Now that you understand these four pillars of success, it's time to take action. Here are powerful strategies to elevate your spiritual success and, by extension, your overall life success:

1. Cultivate Generosity: Open your heart and your hands. Share your wealth, your knowledge, and your positivity. The more you give, the more you'll receive in return.
2. Practice Gratitude: Regularly count your blessings. A thankful heart is a magnet for miracles and a catalyst for lasting success.
3. Believe in Your Worth: Embrace the truth that you deserve success. Your positive attitude is the key that unlocks the door to abundant blessings.
4. Maintain Laser Focus: Success requires unwavering attention and persistence. Nurture your dreams with dedication, and watch them flourish.
5. Embody Respect: Treat others with compassion and openness. Your attitude towards others reflects your self-image and paves the way for mutual success.

The tools for success are within your grasp. Your presence here, engaging with these ideas, proves your commitment to growth and achievement. Don't let fear or procrastination hold you back. Embrace mistakes as learning opportunities, persevere in the face of challenges, and define success on your own terms.

Remember, true success isn't about impressing others or accumulating possessions. It's about achieving genuine happiness across all areas of your life. As you continue this journey, keep pushing your boundaries, never stop learning, and always strive for balance across the four pillars of success.

Success is within your grasp. The tools you need are at your fingertips, waiting to be harnessed. Your presence here, engaging with this book, is a testament to your unwavering commitment to growth and achievement. Remember, learning is the lifeblood of success. When you cease to learn, you risk falling into the trap of complacency, potentially robbing your life of its purpose and meaning.

Procrastination is the silent assassin of dreams. Don't let fear of failure or mistakes paralyze you. Embrace the incredible capacity of your mind to learn from missteps. Each error is a stepping stone, propelling you closer to your goals. Take that first step today – your future self will thank you.

Perseverance is the bedrock of success. It's the unwavering determination that distinguishes achievers from those who fall short. Cultivate resilience, for it is your shield against adversity. When obstacles arise, view them not as barriers, but as opportunities to demonstrate your unwavering commitment to your goals.

True success is measured by happiness, not by others' expectations. Free yourself from the shackles of external validation. Performance anxiety and the constant pursuit of approval have derailed countless talented individuals from reaching their zenith. Your success story is uniquely yours — it cannot be judged by material possessions or others' opinions. The ultimate benchmark of success is your personal fulfillment across all facets of life.

Now, let's embark on a journey of self-discovery. The following questions will help you define your unique vision of success. Armed with this knowledge, the subsequent chapters will serve as your personalized roadmap, guiding you towards your destination on the path to unparalleled achievement.

Are you ready to redefine success and transform your life? The path to extraordinary achievement starts now. Let's embark on this thrilling journey together, unlocking your full potential and creating a legacy of success that will inspire generations to come.

Chapter Work-Up

As we embark on this transformative journey towards success, we invite you to engage in a powerful self-evaluation exercise. The "Chapter Work-Up" sections at the end of each chapter offer a unique opportunity to reflect deeply on the topics presented and apply them to your personal growth. Let's begin with the Chapter Work-Up for Chapter 1, where we'll challenge your perceptions and ignite your passion for success.

In your own words, paint a vivid picture of Success:

_____
_____
_____

Now, contrast that with your definition of Failure:

_____
_____
_____

Who embodies success in your eyes, and why do they inspire you?

_____
_____
_____

Can you identify someone who, despite wealth or fame, you would consider a failure? What valuable lessons can we learn from their story?

_____
_____
_____

Explore the reasons behind society's tendency to equate success with financial status. How can we challenge and expand this narrow definition?

_____
_____
_____

As we forge ahead on our journey to success, it's crucial to map out our current position, our ultimate destination, and the strategic path that will lead us there. This clarity will be the compass guiding us towards our goals.

To maximize the impact of this exercise, we encourage you to record your responses in the reflection journal pages at the end of this chapter. This will create a powerful record of your growth, allowing you to revisit and refine your thoughts as you progress towards your success goals.

Where Are You Today?

1. What aspects of your personal and professional life are thriving?
2. Which areas need improvement or restructuring?
3. What activities or environments bring you joy and fulfillment?
4. What tasks or projects ignite your passion and enthusiasm?
5. Which responsibilities do you find yourself avoiding, and why?
6. What unique strengths set you apart from others?
7. Which areas of personal growth present the greatest opportunities?
8. What skills or abilities do you aspire to develop or enhance?

Where Do You Want to Be?

1. Envision your ideal professional role or career path.
2. Describe your perfect personal life and lifestyle.
3. What core values and principles are non-negotiable for you?

4. Which key relationships do you aim to nurture or establish?
5. List your most ambitious goals, complete with target dates for achievement.
6. Do you see yourself as an entrepreneur or thriving within an organization?
7. What causes or missions ignite your deepest passions?
8. How do you envision making a lasting impact on individuals or communities?
9. In what ways do you aspire to revolutionize your professional field?
10. Beyond basic necessities, what truly motivates and energizes you each day?
11. Prioritize the following factors when considering a new job or career path:

__ Financial Rewards

__ Influence and Authority

__ Intellectual Challenge

__ Professional Development

__ Meaningful Cause

__ Strategic Location

__ Travel Opportunities

__ Dynamic Team Environment

__ Excitement and Enjoyment

__ Career Advancement Prospects

__ Work-Life Balance

__ Leadership Opportunities

How Do You Get There?

The roadmap to your success lies within the pages that follow. We urge you to immerse yourself in each chapter, taking comprehensive notes and diligently completing the work-ups. The insights you gain will be invaluable, serving as stepping stones on your path to greatness. Don't hesitate to revisit key sections, allowing the wisdom to truly sink in and guide your journey. Your commitment to this process is the first step towards realizing your full potential and achieving the success you deserve.

PERFORMANCE JOURNAL

Chapter 2

OVERCOMING FEAR

Fear not! This may seem like an audacious declaration, but let's embrace this powerful emotion and harness its immense potential. Fear, a universal human experience that transcends cultures and generations, can be your greatest ally in achieving success. It's time to reframe our perspective on fear and use it as a catalyst for personal growth, professional achievement, and spiritual development.

Fear is not merely an individual emotion; it can evolve into a potent social force that shapes communities and societies. Like any other emotion, fear moves within us, responding to perceived, sensed, or imagined stimuli. It's deeply rooted in our anticipation of the future and our memories of the past. Fear can be a powerful motivator, preparing us for action and, as the 16th-century French philosopher Michel de Montaigne eloquently stated, capable of transforming "a flock of sheep into an armed squadron." This vivid metaphor illustrates the transformative power of fear when channeled correctly.

Remember, the anticipation of fear is often more detrimental than the actual outcome. As the ancient Roman philosopher Seneca wisely observed, "We suffer more in imagination than in reality." This profound insight reminds us that our minds often magnify our fears beyond their actual proportions. By understanding and embracing fear, you can transform it from a paralyzing force into a driving one, propelling you towards your goals and aspirations.

Let's confront the social aspect of fear - the fear of expectation. Society nurtures expectations for you, but these expectations are often based on limited knowledge and preconceived notions. Your diligent work towards your goals can be a powerful antidote to this fear of the unknown. By focusing on your personal growth and achievements, you can gradually overcome the anxiety associated with societal expectations.

The ancient Greek philosopher Plato asserted that fear, like other emotions, is a motion of the soul. When approached prudently, it can provide foresight and informed opinion, guiding our decisions and actions. In our modern world, as the contemporary sociologist Zygmunt Bauman points out, fear has become a prime mover of human history, signaling modernity's arrival. This perspective highlights the evolving role of fear in shaping our collective experiences and societal structures.

You're living in the most secure society that has ever existed, with unprecedented access to information, technology, and resources. Yet, paradoxically, anxiety and fear persist. It's time to challenge the notion that "failure is not an option" and embrace the empowering mantra "don't let your fear rule you." Take calculated risks, admit inadequacies, and learn from mistakes. This is the path to true growth, success, and personal fulfillment.

Consider the profound wisdom of Steve Jobs, co-founder of Apple Inc., who said, "Remembering that I'll be dead soon is the most important tool I've ever encountered to help me make the big choices in life." This perspective, while seemingly morbid, can be incredibly liberating. It encourages us to focus on what truly matters, freeing us from the chains of fear and empowering us to pursue our passions and purpose with renewed vigor.

Fear is a fundamental survival mechanism, hardwired into our biology through millions of years of evolution. However, it's also an opportunity for tremendous growth. When fear kicks in, it can start your adrenaline pumping, mimicking the chemical effects of positive emotions like happiness and excitement. Embrace this physiological response and channel it into positive action, turning potential threats into opportunities for success.

Take inspiration from legendary figures in sports who turned their failures into stepping stones for success. Consider Babe Ruth, the iconic baseball player who struck out 1,330 times but also hit an impressive 714 home runs. Or Michael Jordan, widely regarded as one of the greatest basketball players of all time, who missed over 9,000 shots and lost nearly 300 games throughout his career. These examples demonstrate that even the most successful individuals face numerous setbacks on their path to greatness.

Failure is not your enemy; it's your greatest teacher. As Thomas Watson, the visionary founder of IBM, advised: "Double your rate of failure... That's where you'll find success. On the far side." This counterintuitive advice encourages us to view failure not as a deterrent, but as a necessary step towards achievement. Embrace this mindset and watch your fear of failure transform into a hunger for growth and innovation.

Your failures are not setbacks; they are "portals of discovery," as the renowned Irish writer James Joyce brilliantly put it. Failure serves multiple purposes in our journey towards success: it softens your approach, develops maturity, broadens thinking, offers invaluable insights, reveals hidden abilities, inspires creativity, reinforces the need for calculated risk-taking, builds courage, opens unexpected opportunities, brings unforeseen benefits, pushes you beyond your perceived limits, and ultimately makes success even sweeter when achieved.

To "fail better," as the acclaimed playwright Samuel Beckett urged, means to fail with purpose and learn from each setback. Truly successful individuals fail much more frequently than they succeed, but they fail well. They don't attach shame or stigma to failure; instead, they treat it as an integral process of growth and learning. Here's how you can adopt this transformative mindset:

- Recognize that failure is not avoidable, a single event, a stigma, the enemy, or final. It's a natural part of any journey towards success.
- Assess your decisions based on what you knew at the time, not with the benefit of hindsight.
- Examine your errors judiciously, considering all circumstances and contextual factors.
- Gather all necessary information to avoid repeating the same mistakes in the future.
- Appreciate constructive feedback and healthy criticism, using them as valuable tools for continuous improvement.

Remember, success is a journey, not a destination. Struggles, confusion, and setbacks are not cause for alarm; they are expected and inevitable parts of your path to greatness. Develop a high tolerance for life's challenges and never let your spirit of inquiry and thirst for knowledge subside. Embrace each obstacle as an opportunity to learn, grow, and become stronger.

Are you ready to embrace failure and turn it into your greatest asset? Reflect on these thought-provoking questions:

- Will you openly share your mistakes and learn from them, fostering a culture of transparency and growth?
- Will you courageously try new things, even when success isn't guaranteed, embracing the unknown?
- Will you view setbacks as opportunities for growth rather than insurmountable obstacles?
- Will you diligently analyze your failures for valuable lessons, treating each one as a learning experience?
- Will you see failure as a stepping stone towards success, not a stumbling block that hinders progress?

If you've answered "Yes" to one or more of these questions, you're already on the path to embracing failure and using it as a powerful tool for success. Remember, each affirmative response represents a commitment to personal growth and resilience.

For those seeking spiritual guidance in their journey to overcome fear, the Bible offers powerful words of encouragement and strength. As stated in 2 Timothy 1:7, "God gave us a spirit not of fear but of power and love and self-control." This verse isn't a call to complacency or inaction, but a powerful reminder of the inner strength and resilience that resides within you, empowering you to face and overcome life's challenges.

Those who trust in a higher power can live fearlessly, drawing strength from their faith! As Psalm 91:5-7 reminds us, "You will not fear the terror of night, nor the arrow that flies by day, nor the pestilence that stalks in darkness, nor the plague that destroys at midday. A thousand may fall at your side, ten thousand at your right hand, but it will not come near you." These words offer comfort and assurance, reinforcing the idea that faith can be a powerful antidote to fear.

Whether you draw strength from religious faith, personal resilience, or the support of others, remember that fear is a natural and universal part of the human experience. The goal isn't to completely eliminate fear, but to harness its power and channel it into positive action. Embrace your fears, learn from your failures, and use them as stepping stones to success. Your journey of overcoming fear starts now - seize it with both hands, let it propel you to new heights of achievement, and watch as you transform challenges into opportunities for growth and success!

PERFORMANCE JOURNAL

Chapter 3
Mastering Stress Management

The ancient Stoic philosopher Epictetus astutely observed, "Whenever I see a person suffering from nervousness, I think, well, what can he expect? If he had not set his sights on things outside man's control, his nervousness would end at once." This profound insight challenges us to reconsider our relationship with stress in an ever-changing world. While we cannot control external factors, we possess the power to revolutionize how we respond to them. This chapter will explore the intricacies of stress, its impact on our lives, and provide you with practical tools to not just manage stress, but to harness it for personal growth and success.

Contrary to popular belief, stress isn't inherently negative. It's your body's remarkable way of protecting you, sharpening your focus, and boosting your energy when you need it most. In emergencies, stress can be your lifeline, providing extra strength to defend yourself. Your heart races, muscles tighten, and senses heighten - preparing you to face challenges head-on. This physiological response, often referred to as the "fight-or-flight" mechanism, has been crucial for human survival throughout our evolutionary history.

However, when stress becomes chronic, it transforms from ally to adversary. The key lies in understanding stress and equipping yourself with powerful tools to manage it effectively. By mastering stress management, you're not just surviving - you're thriving. This shift in perspective can be the difference between feeling overwhelmed by life's challenges and viewing them as opportunities for growth and self-improvement.

Unveiling the Types of Stress: A Comprehensive Overview

To conquer stress, we must first understand its various forms. Each type of stress affects us differently and requires unique management strategies:

1. Eustress: This is the positive stress that ignites motivation and productivity. It's your driving force in high-stakes situations, pushing you to excel. Examples of eustress include the excitement of starting a new job, the thrill of competition, or the anticipation of a joyful event like a wedding. Eustress can enhance performance and personal growth when managed effectively.
2. Distress: This is the negative stress triggered by sudden changes or overwhelming demands. Distress can manifest in several forms:
    - Acute stress: Short-term pressure that can be thrilling in small doses. This could be the adrenaline rush before giving a presentation or the tension felt during a tight deadline. While manageable in small amounts, frequent acute stress can be taxing on the body and mind.
    - Episodic acute stress: Frequent pressure from highly demanding environments. This often affects individuals who take on too many responsibilities or consistently find themselves in high-pressure situations. Over time, this can lead to persistent

anxiety and physical symptoms like headaches or digestive issues.

- Chronic stress: Persistent stress lasting months or years, often due to external factors beyond your control. Examples include ongoing financial difficulties, challenging family dynamics, or prolonged health issues. Chronic stress can have severe long-term effects on both physical and mental health if left unaddressed.

3. Hyper-stress: This refers to the overwhelming pressure when pushed beyond your limits, leading to emotional outbursts and anxiety. Hyper-stress often occurs when individuals face a barrage of stressors simultaneously, leaving them feeling unable to cope. It's crucial to recognize the signs of hyper-stress early to prevent burnout and maintain overall well-being.

4. Hypo-stress: This is the demotivating effect of an unchallenging, monotonous life. While it may seem counterintuitive, a lack of stimulation can be just as stressful as overstimulation. Hypo-stress can lead to boredom, restlessness, and a sense of unfulfillment, potentially impacting mental health and overall life satisfaction.

Your Brain on Stress: A Powerful Ally and Potential Threat

Understanding how your brain responds to stress is crucial for effective management. Your emotional brain, primarily the amygdala, is programmed for survival and triggers the fight-or-flight response. This primal instinct heightens your awareness and prepares your body for action by releasing stress hormones like cortisol and adrenaline. While this can be advantageous in short bursts, providing the energy and focus needed to overcome immediate challenges, chronic stress can wreak havoc on your physical and mental health.

The Challenging Road to Success

Prolonged stress can impair brain function, particularly affecting the prefrontal cortex, which is responsible for decision-making and emotional regulation. It can also damage memory centers like the hippocampus, leading to poor concentration and mood swings. Chronic stress has been linked to a range of health issues, including cardiovascular problems, weakened immune function, and an increased risk of mental health disorders such as anxiety and depression.

But here's the empowering truth: you have the power to manage stress and keep yourself motivated and productive. By understanding the neurological processes behind stress, you can develop strategies to mitigate its negative effects and harness its potential benefits.

Stress Management: Your Path to a Balanced, Resilient Life

Managing stress is about taking charge of your thoughts, emotions, environment, and problem-solving approach. It's not about eliminating stress entirely - which would be both impossible and undesirable - but rather about developing the skills to respond to stress in healthy, productive ways. Your ultimate goal? A balanced life with time for work, relationships, relaxation, and fun, coupled with the resilience to thrive under pressure.

Step 1: Identify Your Stress Sources

Embark on a journey of self-discovery by keeping a stress journal. This powerful tool will help you recognize patterns and address them head-on. Document the following:

- ♦ What triggered your stress?

- How your body reacts to stress - tension in your jaw, itching in your arm, increased heart rate, etc.
- Your emotional response - anger, fear, frustration, etc.
- How you dealt with the stressor
- What helped or didn't help in managing the stress

Over time, this journal will reveal patterns in your stress responses and help you identify the root causes of your stress. This awareness is the first step towards effective stress management.

Step 2: Revolutionize Your Coping Strategies

Once you've identified your stress triggers, it's time to develop healthier coping mechanisms. Ditch unhealthy habits like excessive drinking, overeating, or mindless scrolling. These may provide temporary relief but often exacerbate stress in the long run. Instead, embrace these life-changing strategies:

- Cultivate strong social support: Build and maintain a network of supportive relationships. This can include family, friends, colleagues, or support groups. Social connections act as a buffer against stress and provide emotional support during challenging times.
- Fuel your body with nutrient-rich foods: A balanced diet can significantly boost your resilience to stress. Focus on whole foods, plenty of fruits and vegetables, lean proteins, and healthy fats. Avoid excessive caffeine and sugar, which can exacerbate stress symptoms.

- Master muscle relaxation techniques: Progressive muscle relaxation involves tensing and then relaxing different muscle groups in your body. This practice can help reduce physical tension and promote overall relaxation.

- Make exercise your daily stress-busting ritual: Regular physical activity is one of the most effective stress management tools. It releases endorphins, improves mood, and enhances overall well-being. Aim for at least 30 minutes of moderate exercise most days of the week.

- Prioritize sleep: Adequate sleep is crucial for stress management. Establish a consistent sleep schedule, create a relaxing bedtime routine, and ensure your sleeping environment is conducive to rest.

- Practice assertive communication: Learn to express your needs and feelings clearly and respectfully. This can help address conflicts head-on and reduce stress in relationships and work environments.

- Reframe your thinking: Use cognitive behavioral therapy techniques to challenge and change negative thought patterns. This can involve identifying cognitive distortions, practicing positive self-talk, and developing a more balanced perspective on stressful situations.

- Embrace acceptance: For situations beyond your control, practice acceptance. This doesn't mean giving

The Challenging Road to Success

up, but rather acknowledging reality and focusing your energy on things you can change.

♦ Incorporate mindfulness and meditation: These practices can help you stay grounded in the present moment, reducing anxiety about the future and regrets about the past. Even a few minutes of mindfulness each day can make a significant difference in your stress levels.

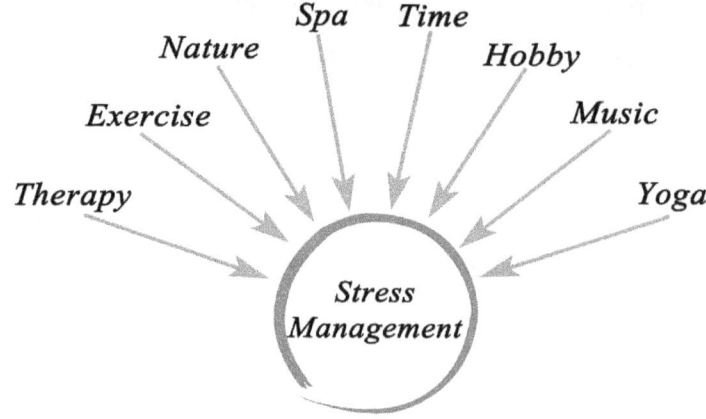

Nurture Your Spirit: The Ultimate Stress Antidote

In times of stress, many find solace and strength in their faith. The Bible offers powerful reassurance and guidance for dealing with life's challenges. Consider this verse from Philippians 4:6-7:

"Do not be anxious about anything, but in everything by prayer and supplication with thanksgiving let your requests be made known to God. And the peace of God, which surpasses all understanding, will guard your hearts and your minds in Christ Jesus."

Let these words wash over you, reminding you that you're never alone in your struggles. God invites you to cast your burdens upon Him, promising rest for your weary soul. This spiritual perspective can provide comfort and a sense of purpose even in the midst of stressful circumstances.

Incorporate spiritual practices into your stress management routine:

- Regular prayer or meditation
- Reading and reflecting on scripture
- Participating in a faith community
- Engaging in acts of service or kindness
- Practicing gratitude

These practices can help you maintain a sense of peace and purpose, even when facing significant challenges.

Your Call to Action: Embrace Stress Management Today

Remember, not all stress is harmful. It's your body's ingenious defense mechanism, designed to help you rise to challenges and grow as an individual. However, chronic stress can be detrimental to both mind and body, potentially leading to serious health issues if left unchecked.

By implementing these powerful stress management techniques, you're not just improving your mood and boosting your immune function - you're potentially saving your life and your relationships. Stress management is a skill that requires practice and patience. Be kind to yourself as you develop these new habits and remember that small, consistent changes can lead to significant improvements over time.

Don't face stress alone. Reach out to friends, family, therapists, or your faith community. You have an army of support ready to help you transform stress from your enemy into your ally. Whether it's talking through your concerns with a trusted friend, seeking professional help from a therapist, or finding strength in your spiritual beliefs, remember that seeking support is a sign of strength, not weakness.

Take the first step today towards a more balanced, resilient, and fulfilling life. Start by choosing one or two stress management techniques to incorporate into your daily routine. Perhaps begin with a simple breathing exercise or a short daily walk. As you become more comfortable, gradually add more strategies to your stress management toolkit.

Your future self will thank you for the investment you're making in your mental, physical, and spiritual well-being. By mastering stress management, you're not just coping with life's challenges - you're setting yourself up to thrive in all aspects of your personal and professional life. Remember, the journey of a thousand miles begins with a single step. Take that step today, and embrace the path to a more balanced, resilient you.

Chapter Work-Up

Empowering Your Stress Journal: A Catalyst for Personal Growth

1. Reflect on today's stress triggers. What sparked anxiety, and how can you transform these challenges into opportunities for growth?
2. Describe your physical and emotional responses to stress. How can understanding these reactions empower you to manage them more effectively?
3. Analyze your stress-induced behaviors. How can you leverage this awareness to develop more constructive coping mechanisms?
4. Identify your most effective stress-relief strategies. How can you amplify and integrate these into your daily routine?
5. Confront your **fears** head-on. What fears are holding you back, and how can you transmute them into powerful catalysts for hope and trust?
6. Uncover the hidden lessons in your current challenges. How can these insights propel you towards personal and professional excellence?

7. Define daily actions that make you feel invincible. How can you prioritize these empowering activities to cultivate unwavering strength?
8. Identify your pillars of support. Who instills calmness and **<u>bravery</u>** in you, and how can you nurture these vital relationships?
9. Celebrate today's triumphs. List five exceptional aspects of your day and consider how to replicate these positive experiences.
10. Target a key area for improvement (e.g., time management, communication). What concrete steps will you take to excel in this domain?
11. Revolutionize your morning routine. What game-changing adjustment will set the tone for an extraordinary day?
12. Transform your evening ritual. What powerful modification will ensure restorative sleep and prepare you for tomorrow's success?
13. Identify a limiting habit or belief. How will releasing this constraint unlock your true potential?
14. Curate your happiness inventory. List ten things that ignite joy in your life and strategize how to incorporate them more frequently.
15. Envision your dream destination. What compelling reasons drive this aspiration, and how can this vision inspire your daily life?

16. Commit to mastering a new skill. What innovative approach will you employ to acquire this valuable asset?
17. Scrutinize areas ripe for enhanced organization. What systems can you implement to maximize efficiency and maintain order?
18. Articulate a long-term goal that ignites your passion. How will achieving this objective transform your life and impact others?
19. Evaluate your progress towards your goals. What bold steps have you taken, or what audacious actions can you implement immediately?
20. Confront your greatest fear. What courageous strategy will you employ to conquer this obstacle and emerge victorious?
21. Analyze challenging days. What valuable lessons can you extract to prevent future setbacks and ensure continuous growth?
22. Dissect a recent problem and your solution. How can you optimize your problem-solving approach for even greater success?
23. Prioritize self-care. How will you create sacred time for relaxation and rejuvenation to fuel your peak performance?
24. Extract wisdom from past mistakes. How will you leverage these hard-earned insights to shape a brighter, more successful future?

25. Craft an inspiring letter to your future self. What powerful vision and unwavering commitment will you convey to your evolved self?

PERFORMANCE JOURNAL

Chapter 4

RESILIENCE

Adversity is not merely a test; it's a transformative opportunity to forge your spirit, sharpen your mind, and strengthen your body. While it may seem indifferent or temporary, adversity serves as the crucible in which true champions are molded. The pivotal question that arises is: Do you possess the psychological resilience necessary to respond swiftly and constructively to crises?

When facing adversity, two distinct paths emerge. The first, all too human and regrettably common, is to assign blame to others - an easy escape that ultimately stunts personal growth and development. The second, far more powerful and rewarding, is through cultivating resilience. By consciously choosing the path of resilience, you gain profound insights into handling life's most challenging moments. This journey of resilience teaches you the invaluable lessons of forgiveness, both for yourself and others, and helps you discover the grace to persevere even in the darkest, most trying times.

This journey towards resilience isn't easy; it's fraught with challenges and obstacles. However, it's through the process of overcoming adversity that you build unshakeable character. While avoiding challenges may seem tempting, offering temporary relief from discomfort, it ultimately robs you of the opportunity for spiritual and psychological growth. Embrace adversity, for it is the forge that tempers the virtues of courage and grace within you, shaping you into a stronger, more resilient individual.

Your response to adversity is a choice - and it's crucial to choose wisely. In the chapters ahead, we'll delve deeper into pain management techniques and methods to build physical toughness. But first, let's equip you with the essential tools to cultivate resilience in the face of adversity. Remember, this book serves as your comprehensive, step-by-step guide to mental mastery, meticulously crafted under the expert guidance of certified sport psychology and stress management coaches. Our mission? To arm you with the knowledge, mental acuity, and practical strategies to triumph over any circumstance in your athletic or professional life. Are you ready to embark on this transformative journey towards unshakeable resilience?

Why is resilience crucial?

Resilience is your superpower - the remarkable ability to rebuild and grow stronger from adversity. In the unpredictable and often tumultuous world of sports and high-performance environments, momentum can shift in the blink of an eye. While you can't control these sudden shifts, you can absolutely control your reaction to them. Adversity is inevitable in any worthwhile pursuit, but it's your response that separates the champions from the rest.

Injuries and illnesses are common hurdles in sports and life, often appearing at the most inopportune moments. Your capacity to bounce back, both physically and mentally, is determined by your level of resilience. Paradoxically, it's in the most challenging times that you build this invaluable trait. As the legendary basketball player Michael Jordan wisely said, "Obstacles don't have to stop you. If you run into a wall, don't turn around and give up. Figure out how to climb it, go through it, or work around it." This quote encapsulates the essence of resilience - the unwavering determination to find a way forward, no matter the obstacle.

Resilient performers are masters of swift action. They rapidly shift from feeling like victims of circumstance to becoming architects of their own success, crafting innovative plans of action. When adversity strikes, they pivot seamlessly from cause-oriented thinking to response-oriented thinking, laser-focused on moving forward and finding solutions. These resilient individuals never stop competing, even in the face of seemingly insurmountable setbacks.

Numerous studies in psychology and sports science have shown that your reaction to stressful situations depends largely on the degree of control you believe you can exercise. But here's the empowering truth: resilience is not an innate, fixed trait, but rather a skill you can develop and strengthen over time. There are numerous techniques and strategies to build your resilience and overcome adversity, each directly linked to your mindset and approach to challenges. Let's explore some powerful strategies to cultivate and enhance your resilience:

1. Reframe the situation: Instead of viewing adversity as an insurmountable obstacle, consciously choose to see it as a challenge to overcome and grow from. This shift in perspective can transform your approach to difficulties.
2. Take responsibility: Rather than blaming external factors or circumstances beyond your control, focus on what you can influence and improve. This empowers you to take action and make positive changes.
3. Identify the scope: Determine if the issue at hand is specific to a particular situation or more widespread.

This assessment allows you to develop targeted, effective solutions.

4. Assess the timeline: Consider whether you're facing a short-term setback or a long-term challenge. Your approach and strategies should match the duration and intensity of the adversity you're facing.
5. Develop a growth mindset: Embrace challenges as opportunities for learning and improvement. View failures not as definitive endpoints, but as valuable feedback for future success.
6. Build a support network: Surround yourself with positive, supportive individuals who can offer encouragement, advice, and different perspectives during difficult times.
7. Practice self-care: Maintain your physical and mental health through regular exercise, proper nutrition, adequate sleep, and stress-management techniques like meditation or deep breathing exercises.
8. Set realistic goals: Break down larger challenges into smaller, manageable tasks. This approach helps maintain motivation and provides a sense of progress and accomplishment.

Remember, grit, perseverance, and resilience aren't genetic traits that some people are born with and others lack. They're skills developed through intentional daily practice and consistent effort. By honing these qualities, you'll be ready to tackle any setback head-on, transforming obstacles into opportunities for growth and success.

Self-regulation: The cornerstone of mental toughness

Self-regulation is the beating heart of sport psychology and a critical component of resilience. It's your ability to control your thoughts, emotions, and motivations, even in high-pressure situations. On the field, when a questionable call ends your chance at bat, or in the boardroom when a crucial presentation doesn't go as planned, your next decision reflects your capacity for self-regulation. Remember, being resilient is a choice - your choice in how you react to adversity.

Developing strong self-regulation skills involves several key practices:

- Mindfulness: Regular mindfulness meditation can help you become more aware of your thoughts and emotions, allowing you to respond rather than react to challenging situations.
- Emotional Intelligence: Work on recognizing and understanding your emotions and those of others. This awareness can help you manage your responses more effectively.
- Stress Management: Develop techniques to manage stress, such as deep breathing exercises, progressive muscle relaxation, or engaging in physical activity.

- Goal Setting: Set clear, achievable goals and create action plans to reach them. This provides direction and motivation, even when facing obstacles.

Visualization: Your mental rehearsal for success

Visualization is your secret weapon in preparing for inevitable challenges. Picture yourself reacting calmly to a bad call, potential injury, or any other setback you might encounter. This mental rehearsal not only prepares you for specific scenarios but also builds your overall resilience, equipping you to handle unforeseen obstacles with grace and composure.

To make your visualization practice more effective:

- Be as detailed as possible in your mental imagery, engaging all your senses.
- Visualize both the process of overcoming challenges and the successful outcome.
- Practice visualization regularly, ideally daily, to strengthen your mental resilience.
- Combine visualization with positive self-talk to reinforce your confidence and determination.

Your support network: The power of positive influence

Surround yourself with positive, supportive individuals who listen without judgment and empathize with your struggles. These pillars of strength will help you cultivate a mindset that views obstacles as stepping stones to success, not roadblocks. A strong support network can provide emotional support, practical advice, and different perspectives on challenges you face.

To build and maintain a robust support network:

- Cultivate relationships with individuals who share your values and goals.
- Be open to receiving help and support when needed.
- Offer support to others in return, creating a reciprocal network of encouragement.
- Consider joining professional associations or support groups related to your field or interests.

Goal recalibration: Adapting to new realities

When adversity strikes, it's time to reassess and adjust your goals. If you lose your playing position, face a career setback, or encounter any significant change in circumstances, reset your objectives to match your new reality and fuel your desire to compete and succeed. Remember Bruce Lee's timeless wisdom: "Be like water." Adapt, flow around obstacles, and use every perceived setback as an opportunity to create positive energy and momentum.

Effective goal recalibration involves:

- Regularly reviewing and adjusting your goals based on current circumstances.
- Breaking down larger goals into smaller, achievable milestones.

- Maintaining flexibility in your approach while staying committed to your overall vision.
- Celebrating small wins along the way to maintain motivation and momentum.

Strive for excellence, but remember that perfection is an unrealistic and often counterproductive measure of success. Give yourself permission to make mistakes - they're valuable learning opportunities that contribute to your growth and resilience. As the renowned author and poet Maya Angelou wisely said, "When you know better, you do better." This perspective allows you to view setbacks as stepping stones to improvement rather than failures.

The Challenging Road to Success

When you experience those uplifting "heck, yeah!" moments of success or breakthrough, pause to lock them into your memory. These positive experiences will be your emotional fuel when times get tough. Cultivate mental cues or anchors to help you revisit these empowering states of mind when you need them most. This practice of savoring positive experiences can significantly boost your resilience and overall well-being.

Remember, failure is feedback. Each setback is an opportunity to build your mental muscle and overcome anxiety. Embrace adversity as your training ground for developing unshakeable resilience. By reframing challenges in this way, you transform obstacles into opportunities for growth and self-improvement.

A Winning System for Overcoming Adversity

Here's a powerful system I share with my players to conquer failure and adversity. This system can be adapted to any sport, job, or performance scenario:

1. Take a breath: Center yourself with deep, controlled breaths, allowing your muscles to relax. This simple act can help you regain composure and assess the situation clearly. Practice diaphragmatic breathing to maximize the calming effect.
2. Use your focal point: Ask yourself: What do I need to do right now? What am I capable of in this moment? Trust in your abilities and prepare to restart. Your focal point could be a physical object, a mantra, or a visualization technique that helps you refocus.
3. Regulate your emotions: Choose your response to stress. Take a moment to reset - remove your glove or hat, take

a deep breath, and regain control. Recognize your emotions without being controlled by them. Practice naming your emotions to create distance and gain perspective.

4. Choose your response: Focus on what you can control - your attitude, effort, thoughts, and emotions. Make your next move a display of excellence. Remember, it's not about the cards you're dealt, but how you play them.

5. Harness your inner strength: Tap into your spiritual reserves. Let grace guide your reactions, allowing you to maintain composure and control in any situation. This could involve prayer, meditation, or connecting with your personal beliefs and values.

COACH TIP: To instill resilience in your performers, lead by example. Show grit, stay late, and push yourself hard. Create safe environments for your performers to fail and learn. This approach helps build a growth mindset in your team. Find the delicate balance between challenging talented players and allowing them to rest on their laurels. Remember, growth occurs at the edge of comfort and challenge.

PARENT TIP: When your child faces obstacles, guide them to review and adjust their goals. Encourage them to maintain a daily routine and practice writing, which can be therapeutic and help organize thoughts. Support them through active listening and patience, allowing them to express their true feelings at home without judgment. Let them struggle with obstacles and help them find solutions - this is the foundation of genuine self-confidence. Remember, your role is to be a supportive guide, not to solve all their problems for them.

Spirituality provides a powerful framework for resilience, offering community and belief in something greater than oneself. Research has shown that regular spiritual practice can have profound effects on mental health, including thickening of the brain's cortex in areas associated with depression and anxiety. This neuroplasticity demonstrates the tangible benefits of spiritual practices on our mental resilience.

Resilience

The Bible offers timeless wisdom on resilience. Isaiah 26:3-4 assures, "You will keep in perfect peace those whose minds are steadfast, because they trust in you. Trust in the LORD forever, for the LORD, the LORD himself, is the Rock eternal." These words remind us of the strength we can draw from faith, providing a stable foundation during turbulent times.

Remember, resilience is not just about bouncing back - it's about bouncing forward. It's about using adversity as a springboard for growth, learning, and ultimate triumph. By combining mental training, grit, discipline, and spiritual grace, you can transcend any challenge and compete at your highest level, even in the face of adversity.

Developing resilience is an ongoing process, not a destination. It requires consistent effort, self-reflection, and a willingness to learn from every experience. As you continue to face and overcome challenges, your resilience will grow stronger, enabling you to handle increasingly difficult situations with grace and determination.

Are you ready to unlock your true potential and become unstoppable in the face of any obstacle? The journey to unshakeable resilience starts now. Let's embrace the challenge together and transform adversity into your greatest advantage! Remember, every setback is an opportunity for a comeback, and with the right mindset and tools, you can turn any obstacle into a stepping stone towards your goals.

Chapter Work-Up

Building Your Resilience: A Transformative Plan

Embark on a journey to fortify your inner strength and unlock your full potential. This powerful resilience-building plan will equip you with the tools to not only withstand life's challenges but to thrive in the face of adversity. Are you ready to discover the resilient leader within you?

1. Recognize Your Stress Signals
   - Where does stress manifest in your body? Pinpoint these areas to gain control.
   - Identify your stress-induced habits. What behaviors signal your discomfort?
2. Forge Physical Resilience

Commit to three life-changing improvements in your daily routine:

1. _____
2. _____
3. _____

Share these commitments with an accountability partner to ensure success!

3. Master the Art of Relaxation

Cultivate a "calm body, calm mind" approach:

List three stress-busting activities for home:

1. _____
2. _____
3. _____

Identify three work-friendly relaxation techniques:

1. _____
2. _____
3. _____

Explore powerful relaxation strategies:

- Embrace mindfulness meditation
- Engage your senses for instant calm:
  - Touch: Hold something comforting
  - Smell: Inhale soothing scents
  - Sight: Gaze at calming images
  - Sound: Listen to tranquil music
  - Taste: Savor a moment of indulgence

4. Harness Your Inner Strength

Reflect on a time you conquered a major challenge:

- What did this experience reveal about your character?
- Which personal strengths propelled you to success?
- Visualize yourself at your most resilient. What does this image tell you?
- How can you leverage these strengths in your current situation?

5. Celebrate Your Triumphs

List your five greatest accomplishments:

1. _____
2. _____
3. _____
4. _____
5. _____

Let these achievements fuel your confidence and drive!

6. Find Meaning in Every Day

Identify the moments and activities that bring purpose to your life. How can you incorporate more of these into your routine?

7. Reframe Your Thoughts

When stress strikes, challenge your thinking:

- What's the worst-case scenario? Can you overcome it?
- What's the best possible outcome?
- What advice would you give a friend in your situation?

8. Draw Inspiration

Recall words of encouragement from a mentor, coach, or hero. Display this powerful message where you'll see it daily, fueling your resilience and self-belief.

The Challenging Road to Success

By embracing this resilience-building plan, you're not just preparing for challenges - you're positioning yourself to excel in sports, business, and life. Your journey to becoming an unstoppable force starts now. Are you ready to unleash your full potential?

PERFORMANCE JOURNAL

Chapter 5

MOTIVATION

Motivation is the catalyst for change, igniting the energy and drive necessary for personal growth and success. As an athlete, you're not merely pursuing a hobby; you're embarking on an extraordinary journey that demands unwavering commitment and dedication. The ancient Greek philosopher Epictetus challenges us with a profound question: "How long will you wait to demand the best for yourself?" This isn't simply a rhetorical inquiry; it's a powerful call to action, urging you to seize your potential and transform your life in ways you may have never imagined possible.

An athlete's life is far from ordinary - it's a path of relentless pursuit and self-discovery. Epictetus reminds us that "the contest is now, you are at the Olympic Games." This metaphor emphasizes that every day presents a unique opportunity to push your limits and redefine what's possible. Your progress isn't measured in years or even months, but in moments - each decision, each practice session, each competition shaping your destiny and molding you into the athlete you aspire to be.

Why do you dedicate countless hours to your sport? What drives you to push through pain, fatigue, and seemingly insurmountable setbacks? Your motivation is your compass, guiding every action and decision you make on and off the field. It's visible in your unwavering focus during grueling training sessions, your passionate engagement in competitions, and your relentless pursuit of excellence in every aspect of your athletic journey. Your behavior, your persistence, your decisiveness - these are the tangible manifestations of the fire that burns within you, fueling your passion for your sport.

Motivation

To harness the power of motivation effectively, it's crucial to identify your core motivations and tap into them daily. Whether you're driven by the thrill of competition, the pursuit of personal bests, or the noble desire to inspire others through your athletic achievements, it's essential to connect with these powerful forces regularly. As the renowned motivational speaker Zig Ziglar wisely said, "People often say motivation doesn't last. Well, neither does bathing - that's why we recommend it daily." Make motivation a habit, a daily practice that fuels your journey to greatness and keeps you focused on your ultimate goals.

Successful elite athletes aim for self-actualization, the pinnacle of psychologist Abraham Maslow's Hierarchy of Needs. They understand that true excellence requires nurturing not just physical prowess, but also psychological, emotional, and spiritual well-being. Your motivation can be both intrinsic and extrinsic, each playing a crucial role in your development as an athlete and as a person.

Intrinsic motivation, that inner fire that comes from within, often propels you with unmatched force. It's the voice in your head that turns setbacks into comebacks, that pushes you to practice harder after a disappointing performance. This internal drive is what gets you out of bed for early morning training sessions and keeps you focused on your long-term goals. Extrinsic motivation, while external, can be equally powerful in shaping your athletic journey. The rush of celebrating a hard-fought win with your team, the desire to make your coach proud, or the dream of standing on

Motivation

an Olympic podium - these external factors can drive you to new heights and push you beyond what you thought possible.

To consistently fuel your motivation and maintain a positive mindset, consider implementing these strategies:

1. Practice positive self-talk relentlessly. Recognize negative thoughts as they arise, consciously banish them from your mind, and replace them with empowering, confidence-boosting affirmations. For example, instead of thinking "I can't do this," train yourself to say "I am capable of overcoming any challenge."
2. Take full responsibility for your thoughts and actions. As the Roman emperor and Stoic philosopher Marcus Aurelius wisely noted, there's a limit to the time assigned to you. Use it wisely to free yourself from limiting beliefs and reach your full potential. This means acknowledging that you have control over your reactions to circumstances, even when you can't control the circumstances themselves.
3. Focus on solutions, not problems. When faced with setbacks or obstacles, immediately ask yourself: "What can I do now to improve this situation and prevent it from happening in the future?" This solution-oriented mindset will help you maintain a positive outlook and continually progress in your athletic journey.

As an elite athlete striving for greatness, make self-actualization your ultimate goal. Embrace these behaviors to help you reach your fullest potential:

- ♦ Approach each day with full concentration and absorption, giving your undivided attention to every task and training session.

Motivation

- Trust your instincts and experiences over popular opinion, recognizing that you know your body and capabilities better than anyone else.
- Pursue honesty and authenticity in all aspects of life, both on and off the field, building a reputation for integrity.
- Stand firm in your convictions, even if they're unpopular, demonstrating the courage to be true to yourself and your values.
- Take responsibility for your actions and work tirelessly towards your goals, understanding that success comes from consistent effort and dedication.
- Identify and courageously confront your defense mechanisms, addressing any psychological barriers that may be holding you back from reaching your full potential.

Remember, your journey as an athlete is not just about physical prowess - it's a spiritual quest for excellence that encompasses all aspects of your being. The Bible offers timeless wisdom to guide you, especially in moments of doubt or exhaustion. As stated in Philippians 4:8, "Whatever is true, whatever is noble, whatever is right, whatever is pure, whatever is lovely, whatever is admirable - if anything is excellent or praiseworthy - think about such things." Let this profound advice guide your thoughts and actions, particularly when faced with challenges or distractions that threaten to derail your focus.

The Challenging Road to Success

Your motivation, ultimately, should stem from a desire for peace with God, to embrace His grace and hope in every aspect of your athletic journey. The book of Proverbs offers beautiful guidance in this regard. Proverbs 3:1-4 states, "My son, do not forget my teaching, but keep my commands in your heart, for they will prolong your life many years and bring you peace and prosperity. Let love and faithfulness never leave you; bind them around your neck, write them on the tablet of your heart. Then you will win favor and a good name in the sight of God and man." These words remind us that true success and fulfillment come not just from athletic achievements, but from living a life of integrity, faith, and devotion.

Motivation

Embrace these words of wisdom, let them fuel your motivation, and propel you towards greatness both in your sport and in your character. As the legendary baseball manager Tommy Lasorda said, "The difference between the impossible and the possible lies in a man's determination." Your determination, coupled with unwavering faith and positive motivation, will be the driving force behind your success. It will carry you through the toughest training sessions, the most challenging competitions, and the inevitable setbacks that are part of any athletic journey.

Now, armed with this understanding of motivation and its crucial role in your athletic pursuits, go forth with renewed vigor. Push your limits, challenge your perceived boundaries, and strive to achieve the extraordinary. Remember that each day is an opportunity to grow, to improve, and to move closer to your goals. Embrace the journey, relish the challenges, and let your motivation be the fire that propels you to heights you've only dreamed of. Your potential is limitless, and with the right motivation, there's no telling what you can achieve!

The Challenging Road to Success

PERFORMANCE JOURNAL

Chapter 6
CONFIDENCE

The Bible, in Proverbs 28:1 (ESV), declares: "The righteous are as bold as a lion." This powerful metaphor encapsulates the essence of true confidence - a trait that not only elevates your performance but transforms you into a better person. Imagine possessing the courage and strength of a lion in every aspect of your life. That's the power of confidence.

Consider this: How much effort have you truly invested in your work? What does your conscience whisper to you in moments of quiet reflection? Only you know the truth. As we delve deeper into this book, particularly in Chapter 9 on ethics, you'll discover how each chapter intertwines, guiding you on an transformative journey towards excellence in both performance and character.

If you've embraced the value of work ethic, instilling it deep within your core, you've laid the foundation for a clear conscience. This clarity breeds an unshakeable confidence that enables you to stand tall in the face of any challenge. But why is confidence so crucial? Why does it permeate every facet of your life?

Confidence is the catalyst that ignites belief. It's the unwavering faith in yourself that propels you to honor commitments, push boundaries, and consistently deliver your best. Can you imagine the ripple effect of your confidence-fueled performance? It's contagious, inspiring those around you and elevating entire teams to unprecedented heights. Picture a team where every member performs as if they're the star player - that's the dream team born of collective confidence.

As a professional trainer, I challenge my team with a simple yet powerful exercise. I gather them and ask, "Who among you is the best player on this team?" The only acceptable answer? A resounding "I AM" from each and every individual. This isn't arrogance; it's the embodiment of true confidence.

Why begin this chapter with biblical wisdom? Because it illuminates the path to genuine confidence with crystal clarity. Even scientific luminaries like Sir Isaac Newton recognized the profound authenticity within scripture, stating, "We account the scriptures of God to be the most sublime Philosophy. I find more sure marks of authenticity in The Bible than in any profane history whatsoever."

Let's delve deeper into the philosophy of 'I AM'. This concept, explored further in the 'Confidence' chapter of The Mental Training Guide For Elite Athletes, underscores the critical importance of a trained mind. It echoes Rene Descartes' famous declaration, "I think, therefore I am" - a fundamental truth that forms the bedrock of self-awareness and confidence.

Descartes, a brilliant mathematician, scientist, and philosopher, sought to address the problem of false beliefs and establish a foundation for true knowledge. His journey teaches us that even the most confident individuals may face moments of doubt. But it's in overcoming these doubts that true confidence is forged.

As mere mortals, we're susceptible to doubts that can cloud our judgment. But remember: "I think" implies the immediate, certain knowledge of one's existence. It's the spark that ignites belief, dispels doubt, and lays the groundwork for unwavering confidence.

When you think, "I can become the best athlete," you're planting the seeds of confidence within yourself.

And how does faith intertwine with this journey towards confidence? For those who believe, there's comfort in knowing that God wouldn't allow routine deception when objectives are clearly understood. This divine assurance can further bolster your confidence.

Believe in yourself. This is the essence of "I Am" in "The Mental Training Guide". Confidence is not just a skill; it's the fundamental cornerstone of a fulfilling life. The confidence you cultivate doesn't just elevate your performance - it strengthens your relationships, balances your life, and shapes you into a more complete human being.

But let's be clear: we're advocating for true, positive confidence - not foolish arrogance. As Proverb 14:16 (JUB) reminds us, "The wise man fears and departs from evil, but the fool rages and is confident." True confidence is grounded in wisdom and self-awareness.

Confidence

This positive confidence is the launchpad for your Mental Master Method. It's the key that unlocks your potential, allowing you to understand yourself better, clarify your motivations, refine your attitude, and pursue your goals with unwavering determination.

Remember, genuine confidence isn't built on external validation or fleeting successes. It's forged through honest effort, resilience in the face of challenges, and the ability to harness your inner resources to emerge stronger from every setback.

How can you gauge your true confidence? Look for the absence of doubt and uncertainty. Ask yourself: Can you handle the pressure of a crucial moment, even against formidable opponents? Your ultimate goal is an unshakeable mental game, free from the loops of mistakes and negative emotions that can derail your performance.

In mentally demanding sports like baseball, where failure and adversity are constant companions, confidence is your lifeline. It's what prevents a temporary slump from becoming a lasting decline. Your mantra should be 'Nothing Gets by Me'. Fear, doubts, and stress are natural - but with true confidence, you can manage these emotions rather than be overwhelmed by them. Mental training is the key to maintaining this control.

Ready to build your confidence? Here are powerful mental training hacks to get you started:

1. Embrace relentless persistence: Decide that you will never stop striving. This unwavering commitment breeds self-satisfaction and an unstoppable mindset.
2. Adopt a "never lose" philosophy: While losses may occur, this mindset ensures they're merely fleeting moments in your journey of continuous improvement.
3. Always look forward: Keep your mind laser-focused on overcoming challenges and constant self-improvement.
4. Eliminate procrastination: When an opportunity to progress towards your goals arises, seize it immediately. Prioritize ruthlessly.
5. Maintain constant motion: Take consistent, purposeful action that drives you forward.

For coaches, supervisors, and parents supporting performers: Remember that technique isn't always the answer. Sometimes, it's about addressing the mind behind the skill. Offer calm, one-on-one counsel when anxiety or fear strikes. Parents, focus on nurturing independent, decision-making adults. Be attentive listeners and supportive guides.

Confidence is your essential equipment - as crucial as cleats are to a baseball player.

Let's draw inspiration from the timeless wisdom of the Bible:

Hebrews 6:11-20 (NIV) urges us: "We want each of you to show this same diligence to the very end, so that what you hope for may be fully realized. We do not want you to become lazy, but to imitate those who through faith and patience inherit what has been promised."

True confidence blossoms when rooted in faith. Psalm 16 exemplifies this positive confidence in God. It teaches us to attribute our successes to a higher power, basing our hope on unwavering divine character. This perspective liberates us from the burden of expectations, allowing us to focus on the spirit of our endeavors.

Here's what we can learn from this biblical wisdom:

- Faith provides control over anxiety and fear.
- Surrender to a higher purpose brings peace and focus.
- Obedience to principled guidance helps redirect unhelpful thoughts.
- Gratitude for overcoming adversity strengthens resilience.

Joshua 1:9 (ESV) reminds us: "Have I not commanded you? Be strong and courageous. Do not be frightened, and do not be dismayed, for the Lord your God is with you wherever you go."

The Bible also emphasizes the importance of wisdom in cultivating true confidence. It's through wisdom that we stand firm in our convictions and efforts.

Let these powerful words guide and inspire you:

- ♦ God gives hope to the needy (Psalm 9:18, ESV).
- ♦ No one who hopes in You will ever be put to shame (Psalm 25:3, NIV).
- ♦ May I never forget Your words, for they are my only hope (Psalm 119:43, TLB).

Embrace these teachings, cultivate true confidence, and watch as you transform into the best version of yourself - in sports, business, and life.

PERFORMANCE JOURNAL

Chapter 7
CONSISTENCY: THE CORNERSTONE OF EXCELLENCE

Aristotle's profound wisdom resonates through the ages: "We are what we repeatedly do. Excellence, then, is not an act, but a habit." This timeless insight illuminates the immeasurable value of consistency in our lives. To truly harness its power, we must delve deeper into understanding how our brain functions and how consistency shapes our decision-making process.

Recent research reveals that our past judgments significantly influence our perception when making decisions. This fascinating discovery sheds light on how we arrive at conclusions and underscores the critical importance of instilling habits that align positively with our goals. By doing so, we can avoid falling prey to consistency bias while leveraging the brain's natural tendencies to our advantage.

Consistency bias, often manifested as the "I-knew-it-all-along" attitude, can lead to irrational behavior if left unchecked. As Adam Smith astutely observed in "The Theory of Moral Sentiments," "The opinion which we entertain of our own character depends entirely on our judgments concerning our past conduct. It is so disagreeable to think ill of ourselves, that we often purposely turn away our view from those circumstances which might render the judgment unfavorable." This profound insight emphasizes the need for self-awareness and honest self-reflection in our pursuit of consistency.

Consistency: The Cornerstone of Excellence

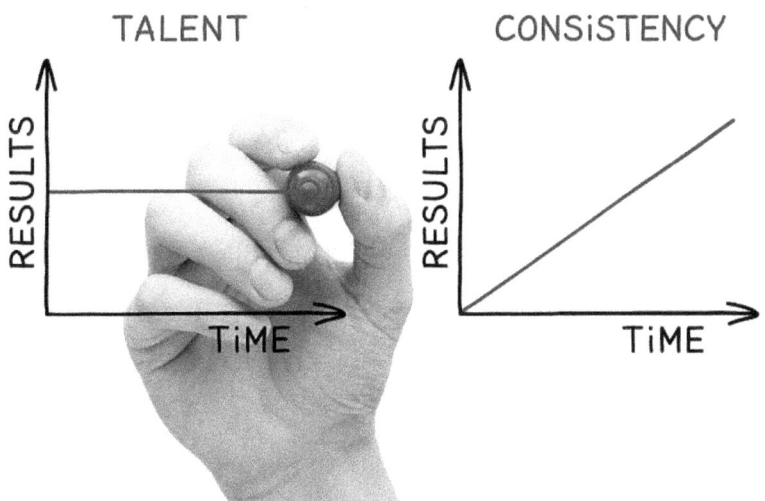

The power of consistency lies in its ability to shape our future selves. By aligning our thoughts, actions, and habits with our goals,

we create a formidable force for personal growth and achievement. However, we must exercise wisdom in our pursuit of consistency, avoiding the trap of foolish persistence in unproductive routines.

Envision your future self. Is this vision aligned with your current performance? Does it reflect your rationality, honesty, and hard work? To bridge the gap between your present and future self, you must harmonize your brain's processes with the relentless effort required to realize that vision. This demands openness to constructive feedback, a willingness to embrace new challenges, and the courage to adapt when necessary.

As Ralph Waldo Emerson wisely cautioned, "Imitation is suicide." True consistency isn't about rigidly adhering to outdated methods or blindly following others. It's about maintaining unwavering commitment to your goals while remaining flexible in your approach. If changing your pitching style can make it more effective, embrace that change. Consistency is about the steadfast pursuit of excellence, not the stubborn clinging to ineffective habits.

Imagine consistency as the daily discipline of meditation followed by focused practice, regardless of your emotional state. It's the commitment to journaling your experiences, both positive and negative, and actively working to improve. Consistency doesn't mean maintaining an ineffective batting style; it means persistently seeking ways to enhance your performance.

Your brain, processing thousands of decisions daily based on sensory input, subconsciously conditions itself according to the stimuli it receives. By consciously cultivating intellectual honesty and positive habits, you can harness this conditioning power to maintain a positive self-image and drive continuous improvement.

Consistency generates consistency. Success in motion stays in motion. Treat your mind like a finely-tuned machine, neither overworking it into duress nor allowing it to rust from disuse. Remain steady in your hard work, focusing on the process rather than fixating solely on the end goal. As Ernest Hemingway famously said, "I write one page of masterpiece to ninety-one pages of crap daily. I try to put the crap in the wastebasket." This unwavering commitment to the craft, regardless of immediate results, epitomizes true consistency.

Embrace consistency as a powerful tool to alleviate pressure and avoid the pitfalls of perfectionism. As an athlete, you naturally strive for excellence, but expecting every performance to be stellar can be overwhelming. Consistency acts as a filter, allowing you to refine your game incrementally, preparing you for those crucial moments when peak performance matters most.

Consistency provides invaluable insight into your capabilities and areas for improvement. It enables you to set and achieve realistic small goals, steadily building towards larger accomplishments. Sporadic, grandiose displays of preparation cannot replace the deep understanding and growth that come from consistent, dedicated practice.

There's an ethical value inherent in consistency that cannot be overstated. By internalizing consistency as a core principle, alongside honesty and integrity, you become reliable, credible, and trustworthy in the eyes of your teammates, coaches, and supporters. This ethical foundation provides a buffer of respect and positive motivation, even when facing temporary setbacks or slumps.

Inconsistency, while sometimes yielding short-term results, leaves you vulnerable to sudden breakdowns and erosion of trust. As noted by the Harvard Business Review, "Values can set you apart. But coming up with strong values—and sticking to them—requires real guts." This rings especially true for those in leadership positions, where consistent behavior becomes a cornerstone of reliability and capability.

Remember: consistent sub-par performance is often preferable to brilliant but erratic results. Teammates and coaches can adapt to and work with consistency, even if it's not perfect. Unpredictability, on the other hand, breeds uncertainty and undermines team cohesion.

To achieve true excellence, strive for consistency in your performance, avoiding wild swings between brilliance and mediocrity. Set clear, consistent expectations for yourself, hold yourself accountable for mistakes, and continually work on addressing your weaknesses. The more consistent you become, the stronger the connection between reliability, credibility, and trust will grow, leading to better outcomes and greater satisfaction for both you and those around you.

Consistency frees you from constraining contradictions. It harmonizes your ethical principles with your actions, allowing you to live authentically and rationally. When faced with conflicting desires or values, work to shape your internal landscape, creating a harmony that aligns with your deepest convictions and aspirations.

To cultivate consistency in your life:

- Clarify your values and remain steadfast in upholding them.
- Strengthen your spiritual integrity to align with your beliefs.
- Respond reliably to challenges, setting realistic goals and bouncing back from setbacks.
- Establish a realistic, flexible daily routine that accommodates growth and change.
- Create appropriate mental rules, phrasing them positively and reminding yourself of them regularly.
- Instill positive behaviors implicitly, celebrating small victories to build a sense of accomplishment.
- Practice mindfulness, staying present and avoiding rigidity or excessive self-pressure.

The Challenging Road to Success

The Bible offers profound insights into the power of persistence and consistency. The Parable of the Persistent Widow (Luke 18:1-8) teaches us the value of unwavering determination. Just as the widow's persistence brought her justice, your consistent efforts will yield desired results in your personal and professional life.

Ethical behavior, at its core, is a matter of consistency—extending to all persons the same respect and consideration we claim for ourselves. As Matthew 7:12 succinctly puts it, "Do unto others as you would have them do unto you: this is the whole Law and the prophets."

God's nature, plans, and purpose remain constant, offering a model of perfect consistency. As Malachi 3:6 declares, "I the Lord do not change." This divine consistency extends to His plans for salvation and His promises to His people. By emulating this steadfast nature, we can cultivate a life of purpose, integrity, and lasting impact.

As you embark on your journey of consistent growth and achievement, remember that your plans should align with God's will. Seek His guidance and nourishment for your soul. Psalm 33:11 reminds us, "But the plans of the Lord stand firm forever, the purposes of his heart through all generations."

In conclusion, let us commit to a life of purposeful consistency, evolving together in pursuit of excellence, guided by timeless wisdom and unwavering faith. Through consistent effort, ethical behavior, and alignment with divine principles, we can achieve greatness in sports, business, and life.

The Challenging Road to Success

PERFORMANCE JOURNAL

Chapter 8
MEDITATION AND MINDFULNESS - UNLOCKING YOUR MENTAL POTENTIAL

Before the first pitch is thrown, before the starting whistle blows, a game can be won or lost in the athlete's mind. Your greatest opponent? It's not the person across the field or on the other side of the net - it's yourself. Victory is only possible when you're emotionally at peace, acutely aware of your thoughts, feelings, and behaviors. This state of mindfulness, this profound self-awareness, frees you from the shackles of past regrets and future anxieties, restoring your being with self-love and kindness. But how can you achieve this transformative state that seems so elusive to many?

As promised in our exploration of Motivation, we now delve into the powerful realm of Meditation. John Kabat-Zinn, a pioneer in the field of mindfulness-based stress reduction, eloquently defines meditation as "the awareness that arises through paying attention in a non-judgmental way in the present moment." This practice isn't just a momentary respite from the chaos of daily life; it's a profound tool that elevates your consciousness, cultivating compassion, love, patience, and mindfulness. Think of mindfulness as meditation's mirror, focusing your mind on specific objects, thoughts, or activities to maintain a stable emotional state. It's the art of being fully present, engaged in the here and now, rather than dwelling on the past or worrying about the future.

Meditation is not just a practice; it's a way of cultivating your mind, of tending to the garden of your thoughts with care and intention. With persistence and dedication, you'll find yourself mindful in every action, even in the simple act of walking. This heightened awareness can elevate your thoughts to extraordinary levels, allowing you to perceive the world around you with newfound clarity and insight. Meditation brings you to your right mind, your still mind - a place of calm amidst the storm of daily life. In a world full of distractions, where notifications ping incessantly and demands on our attention never cease, the stillness you cultivate through meditation becomes your steadfast companion, guiding you when the noise becomes unbearable.

As the brilliant physicist Albert Einstein wisely noted, "You can't solve a problem from the same level of thinking that created it." It's time to elevate your level of thinking, to ascend to a higher plane of consciousness, and meditation is your ticket to this transformative journey. By quieting the mind and focusing inward, you create space for new insights, innovative solutions, and a deeper understanding of yourself and the world around you.

Visualization: Your Mental Superpower for Peak Performance

Visualization is a potent mental skill that empowers you to conjure vivid mental images, helping you conquer fear and insecurity. This technique isn't just a feel-good exercise; it's a scientifically proven method used by elite professionals across various fields. Take, for example, Major League Baseball pitcher Jon Lester and golf legend Tiger Woods. Both have harnessed the power of visualization to sharpen their mental game and achieve extraordinary success in their respective sports.

By visualizing high-pressure scenarios and seeing your best moves in your mind's eye, you cultivate in-game confidence and improved performance. It's like creating a mental rehearsal space where you can practice your skills, strategies, and reactions without physical limitations. With consistent effort and practice, you'll witness a remarkable phenomenon: your body complying with the mental images you've created, your muscles reacting as if the visualized scenario were real, and your mind aligning precisely where you want it to be when faced with actual challenges.

Remember, imagination is the genesis of creation. As the brilliant playwright George Bernard Shaw once said, "Imagination is the beginning of creation. You imagine what you desire, you will what you imagine, and at last, you create what you will." This isn't just poetic rhetoric; it's a principle backed by cutting-edge scientific research. Groundbreaking studies from the University of Colorado Boulder and Icahn School of Medical Researchers confirm that "imagination is a neurological reality that can impact your brain and body in ways that matter for your wellbeing."

Fascinatingly, researchers found that real and imagined exposure to threats are indistinguishable at the whole brain level. This explains why dreaming about falling can cause your body to jerk in response - it's one of your body's defense mechanisms kicking in, even though the threat isn't real. Similarly, mental imagery becomes your waking life's defense mechanism, a powerful tool cultivated through your mind to face adversity head-on. By visualizing success, overcoming challenges, and performing at your peak, you're essentially programming your brain and body to respond positively when faced with real-world situations.

Visualization in Action: The Olympic Gold Standard

To truly understand the power of visualization, let's consider the inspiring example of Sally Gunnell, the 1992 Olympic Gold Medalist in 400m hurdles and 1993 World Champion. Gunnell's preparation was not just physical; it was a rigorous mental regimen that set her apart from her competitors. In her own words: "I used to spend hours and hours visualizing each race. Not in a dreamy way, but with loads of detail, every stride, every hurdle, every centimeter of the track. I visualized rain, sun, and wind. I visualized a noisy crowd and a quiet one."

This level of detail in visualization is crucial. Gunnell didn't just imagine herself winning; she meticulously rehearsed every aspect of her performance in her mind. She visualized different weather conditions, varying crowd reactions, and potential obstacles. Her goal? To arrive at the venue unfazed, confident in her ability to handle any situation that might arise. As she put it, "That's okay, I have thought about that. I know what I have to do."

This approach to mental preparation demonstrates the true power of visualization. By repeatedly running through various scenarios in her mind, Gunnell was able to build a reservoir of confidence and preparedness that she could draw upon during the actual event. She wasn't just hoping for success; she had already experienced it countless times in her mind, making the physical act of running the race feel almost like a familiar routine.

Embrace the Power of Visualization: A Step-by-Step Guide

Ready to harness this transformative technique for yourself? Here's a powerful visualization exercise that you can incorporate into your daily routine:

1. Find a quiet, comfortable space where you won't be disturbed. Lie down on your back and gently close your eyes.
2. Take a deep, slow inhale through your nose, feeling your lungs and belly expand with air. Hold this breath for a moment, savoring the sensation.
3. Exhale slowly and deliberately through your mouth, feeling tension leave your body with each breath.
4. On your next inhale, mentally follow the path of the air as it enters your body. Visualize it flowing down your throat, along your back and chest, and into your belly. Feel your muscles relaxing and tension melting away along this path.
5. As you exhale through your mouth, imagine any remaining stress or negative energy leaving your body with the breath.
6. Repeat this breathing cycle, taking your time and focusing your attention on the imagery. There's no need to rush; allow yourself to sink deeper into relaxation with each breath.

7. Once you feel centered and relaxed, begin to visualize yourself performing the activity you want to improve. See yourself executing perfect form, making split-second decisions with confidence, and achieving your goals.
8. Engage all your senses in this visualization. What do you see? What sounds do you hear? Can you feel the texture of your equipment or the ground beneath your feet? What smells are present in your environment? The more vivid and multi-sensory you can make this experience, the more effective it will be.
9. Practice this visualization for 10-15 minutes, or longer if time allows. The key is consistency - try to make this a daily habit.

Remember, this practice isn't just about relaxation - although that's certainly a beneficial side effect. It's about rewiring your brain for success, creating neural pathways that support peak performance. By consistently engaging in visualization, you're training your mind and body to perform at their absolute best when it matters most.

Meditation: Your Path to Peak Performance and Inner Peace

Meditation is paradoxical in nature - it's about the 'stillness of being' in a world that constantly demands action. In meditation, you become an observer of your inner world, applying minimal effort for maximum impact. This practice of mindful awareness can have profound effects on your performance, both on and off the field.

To begin your meditation journey, start with something simple yet powerful. Imagine your favorite color as the focal point of your meditation. Picture this color as a soothing, healing light that envelops you. On the field or court, let the grass beneath your feet or the texture of the ball become your anchor, grounding you in the present moment. Use powerful keywords or phrases like "stay on base" or "focus on the target" to refocus your mind during visualization and actual performance.

When is the best time to practice meditation and visualization? While any time can be beneficial, many athletes find particular value in meditating right after practices or games. This is an ideal opportunity to analyze your performance objectively and visualize improvements while everything is fresh in your mind. By doing this, you're reinforcing positive patterns and addressing areas for improvement in a constructive, non-judgmental way.

Combating High-Pressure Situations: The Scientific Edge of Mindfulness

You might be wondering: can imagery and meditation truly help in high-pressure situations? The answer, backed by rigorous scientific research, is a resounding yes! A groundbreaking study at the University of Massachusetts Centre for Mindfulness revealed fascinating changes in the brains of participants who practiced mindfulness meditation regularly.

IMAGERY

The study found that these participants experienced increased gray-matter density in the hippocampus - a region crucial for learning and memory - and in structures associated with self-awareness, compassion, and introspection. This suggests that meditation doesn't just make you feel calmer; it actually changes the physical structure of your brain in ways that enhance cognitive function and emotional regulation.

Even more compelling for athletes facing high-pressure situations, the study found that participant-reported reductions in stress correlated with decreased gray-matter density in the amygdala. The amygdala is known to play a vital role in anxiety and stress responses, so this reduction suggests that meditation can literally shrink the part of your brain responsible for stress reactions. This scientific evidence underscores the power of meditation in reducing stress and enhancing performance under pressure.

By harnessing visualization and meditation techniques, you can mentally prepare for high-pressure situations, whether it's the bottom of the ninth in the World Series, the final stretch of a marathon, or a crucial business presentation. This mental preparation acclimatizes your mind to real-life high-pressure scenarios, giving you a competitive edge when it matters most. You're not just hoping to perform well under pressure; you're training your brain to remain calm and focused in these situations.

Reverse Visualization: Your Secret Weapon Against Anxiety

For those grappling with performance anxiety - a common challenge for athletes at all levels - reverse visualization can be a game-changing technique. This approach involves embracing failure by imagining worst-case scenarios, which might seem counterintuitive at first. However, by allowing yourself to be okay with making mistakes, you can conquer the fear that holds so many players back.

Here's how to practice reverse visualization:

1. Start by imagining a scenario where you make a mistake or fail to meet your goals.
2. Instead of avoiding these thoughts, lean into them. What's the worst that could happen?
3. Now, visualize yourself responding to this failure with resilience and determination.
4. See yourself learning from the mistake, adjusting your strategy, and coming back stronger.
5. Imagine the support of your teammates, coaches, or loved ones in this moment.
6. Finally, picture yourself moving past this setback and achieving success in future endeavors.

Remember, even the greatest athletes in history have faced failure. Michael Jordan, widely regarded as the best basketball player of all time, missed 26 game-winning shots in his career. Yet, we remember his six NBA championships and countless clutch performances. By practicing reverse visualization, you prepare yourself to bounce back from setbacks, turning potential failures into stepping stones for success.

Breathing and Relaxation: Your On-Demand Performance Enhancers

As the legendary golfer Byron Nelson wisely advised, "One way to break up any kind of tension is good deep breathing." Controlled breathing is a powerful tool that you can use anywhere, anytime to center yourself and manage stress effectively. Here's a simple yet potent exercise you can practice in the privacy of your room or even in the locker room before a big game:

1. Find a comfortable position, either sitting or lying down, and gently close your eyes.
2. Begin to breathe slowly and deeply, focusing your attention on a positive emotion or thought. This could be confidence, strength, or any quality you want to embody.
3. Assign a color to this positive emotion. For example, you might imagine confidence as a warm golden light, or strength as a vibrant blue energy.
4. As you inhale deeply through your nose, visualize this colored energy flowing into your body. Feel it moving past your chest and into your belly, filling you with positive energy.
5. As you exhale slowly through your mouth, imagine any unwanted emotions or tension leaving your body, perhaps as a dark or cloudy color.
6. Continue this cycle of breathing and visualization, allowing yourself to sink deeper into relaxation with each breath.

With every inhale, you're drawing in more of that positive energy, and with every exhale, you're releasing more tension.
7. Practice this for 5-10 minutes, or longer if time allows. The more you practice, the more easily you'll be able to tap into this state of relaxation when you need it most.

This simple yet powerful tool is your key to achieving relaxation and managing stress effectively, even in high-pressure situations. By incorporating these breathing and visualization techniques into your daily routine, you're not just preparing for your next game or performance - you're transforming your entire approach to stress management and peak performance.

Spiritual Meditation: Elevating Your Game and Your Soul

As we explore the realms of meditation and mindfulness, it's crucial to remember that true greatness comes from cultivating not just a disciplined mind, but also a spiritual one. For many athletes and leaders, spiritual meditation provides a profound source of strength, guidance, and inner peace that transcends the physical and mental aspects of performance.

Meditation can be a powerful way to internalize God's Word, allowing the Holy Spirit to guide, teach, purify, and transform you from within. As the Bible reminds us in Matthew 6:6 (NIV), "But when you pray, go into your room, close the door and pray to your Father, who is unseen. Then your Father, who sees what is done in secret, will reward you." This verse emphasizes the importance of creating a quiet, private space for spiritual reflection and connection.

Heed the call in Joshua 1:8 (NIV): "Keep this Book of the Law always on your lips; meditate on it day and night, so that you may be careful to do everything written in it. Then you will be prosperous and successful." This passage underscores the value of consistent spiritual meditation, suggesting that regular reflection on spiritual teachings can lead to both personal growth and worldly success.

As you've learned to visualize your physical performance, now extend that practice to visualize your spiritual growth. Bring your thoughts to a higher consciousness, pondering the wonders of the world around you, within you, and beyond your comprehension. In the simple act of prayer, declare as in Psalm 145:5 (ESV), "On the glorious splendor of your majesty, and on your wondrous works, I will meditate." This practice of spiritual visualization can deepen your faith and provide a wellspring of strength and inspiration.

Why pray? We pray to connect ourselves to the One who manages the entire universe and to align our thoughts and actions with His higher purpose. Prayer is your means of seeing God in other lives, fostering compassion and kindness towards others - and crucially, towards yourself. It's a practice that can help you maintain perspective, find meaning in both victories and defeats, and cultivate a sense of purpose that extends beyond personal achievement.

As you embark on this transformative journey of meditation and mindfulness, let the powerful promise in Isaiah 26:3 (ESV) guide your path: "You keep him in perfect peace whose mind is stayed on you, because he trusts in you." This profound verse not only encapsulates but vividly illustrates the deep, unshakeable peace and unwavering stability that flows from centering your mind on the spiritual.

By embracing this practice, you're not just adopting a technique; you're unlocking a gateway to profound inner tranquility. This isn't merely about finding moments of calm in a chaotic world - it's about cultivating a steadfast, unbreakable connection with the divine that permeates every aspect of your life. As you anchor your thoughts in spiritual truths, watch as anxiety melts away, clarity emerges, and a sense of purpose ignites your soul.

Don't just read these words - experience them. Let this verse become your mantra, your beacon in times of turmoil. The peace promised isn't fleeting or superficial; it's perfect, all-encompassing, and available to you right now. Trust in this promise, center your mind, and step into the transformative power of true spiritual mindfulness today.

PERFORMANCE JOURNAL

Chapter 9
WORK ETHIC – THE CORNERSTONE FOR SUCCESS

(ESV, Romans 8:5-6) proclaims, *"For those who live according to the flesh set their minds on the things of the flesh, but those who live according to the Spirit set their minds on the things of the Spirit."*

Immanuel Kant, one of history's most influential philosophers, argued that only one thing can be considered unconditionally good: a good will. This good will - your intention, your motivation behind completing your task - is the very essence of a strong work ethic. Kant's philosophy emphasizes the importance of moral duty and the intrinsic value of ethical behavior, which aligns closely with the concept of a robust work ethic in both sports and business.

Why should you infuse ETHICS into your daily life? Let's delve deeper into this crucial aspect of personal development, building upon our previous exploration of personality and emotional intelligence. This chapter will illuminate the indispensable values and behaviors you must cultivate to become the most successful performer you can be. By understanding and embracing these ethical principles, you'll not only enhance your performance but also contribute positively to your team, organization, and society at large.

Work ethic encompasses vital traits such as honesty, integrity, humility, dedication, responsibility, preparation, and accountability. These qualities shape your identity, dictate your interactions, and determine your reactions to challenges. They are the building blocks of who you are and who you will become. Embracing a strong work ethic means winning without boasting, persevering through difficulties, and constantly striving for improvement. It's a daily commitment to excellence in thought and action. But how can you cultivate such a powerful work ethic?

Begin by embracing this fundamental principle: Proper Psychological Practice Prevents Poor Performance. These are the 'six Ps of work ethic' that will propel you towards success. This mantra encapsulates the importance of mental preparation and consistent, ethical behavior in achieving peak performance. By focusing on proper psychological practices, you create a foundation for success that goes beyond mere physical ability or talent.

Consider this scenario: The initial excitement of a new season or job has faded. Dishonesty and laziness have crept in, and pride has clouded your judgment. Your once-insatiable appetite for excellence has waned. How did this happen, and more importantly, how can you overcome it? This situation is not uncommon, and recognizing it is the first step towards reclaiming your strong work ethic.

Let's examine your work ethic through a simple test:

If your coach or trainer asks you to do 30 push-ups every morning as soon as your feet hit the floor, do you:

1. Do exactly 30?
2. Push yourself to do a couple more each time?
3. Perform the push-ups in front of an audience for motivation?

4. Complete the push-ups first thing in the morning, focusing on your long-term goals of improved speed, health, and punctuality?

Your response reveals your work ethic:

Average Work Ethic (a): While this approach may suffice temporarily, it won't equip you to overcome significant challenges. Doing the bare minimum might keep you afloat, but it won't propel you towards excellence or help you stand out in competitive environments.

Strong Work Ethic (b): Going the extra mile physically is commendable, but don't neglect mental exercises like gratitude practice to achieve mind-body synergy. This approach shows initiative and a desire to improve, but remember that true growth comes from balancing physical and mental development.

Pretended Work Ethic (c): Seeking the spotlight can distract you from your true goals - don't let vanity overshadow your performance. While external validation can be motivating, it's crucial to develop intrinsic motivation that sustains you even when no one is watching.

Exceptional Work Ethic (d): This mindset sets you up for success, but be vigilant. Guard against burnout from overexertion or compensating for others' shortcomings. Prioritize daily mental training and focus exercises to maintain your edge. This approach demonstrates a holistic understanding of personal development and long-term goal setting.

Remember, as an athlete or business professional, you're always evolving. The key is to cultivate and maintain an exceptional work ethic. Here's how:

Preparation - Embrace the power of repetitive learning. Harness mental elements like positivity, goal-setting, mental toughness, and resilience to fuel your growth. Preparation goes beyond physical readiness; it involves mental and emotional preparation as well. This could include visualization techniques, mindfulness practices, or studying your field to gain a competitive edge.

Dedication - Cultivate an instinct to work harder. Give your undivided attention to your practice. Heed the cautionary tale of

The Challenging Road to Success

Yankees legend Mickey Mantle, who regretted the years he "took off" during his career, preventing him from reaching his full potential. Mantle's story serves as a powerful reminder that talent alone is not enough; consistent dedication is crucial for long-term success.

Don't fall into the trap of complacency. Instead, emulate Hall of Famer Don Mattingly's philosophy: "I want to improve every day in every facet of the game. It's as simple as that." This mindset of continuous improvement is what separates the good from the great in any field.

Responsibility - Master your reactions to both triumphs and setbacks. Here are five powerful strategies to cultivate responsible behavior:

1. Define a clear mission for your performance and practice. For instance, commit to patience and perfect timing in your actions. This could involve setting specific, measurable goals for each training session or workday.
2. Take life one day at a time and approach your game one play at a time. Maintain unwavering self-control. This strategy helps prevent overwhelm and allows you to focus fully on the task at hand.
3. Focus on the process, not just the outcome. Look beyond individual results to see the bigger picture. This approach helps build resilience and maintains motivation even when immediate results aren't visible.

Work Ethic – The Cornerstone for Success

4. Harness the power of mental imagery. Visualize yourself executing flawless plays, making crucial tackles, sinking game-winning shots, or closing major business deals. Regular visualization can improve performance by enhancing muscle memory and boosting confidence.
5. Commit to daily learning. Develop a habit of evaluating each performance to identify areas for improvement. This could involve keeping a journal, seeking feedback from mentors, or analyzing video footage of your performance.

Identify Work Ethic Boosters and Suckers

While downtime with friends is essential, beware of those constantly in "downtime mode" - they can erode your work ethic. During critical training periods, surround yourself with energetic, positive individuals. Don't let others' lack of work ethic affect your drive. The people you associate with can significantly impact your motivation and performance, so choose your company wisely.

What if family members become work-ethic suckers? Create and fiercely protect your own environment, both physically and mentally. Establish boundaries to safeguard your work ethic. Treat your mindset like a sacred space - guard it vigilantly against negative influences, including your own self-doubts. This might involve having honest conversations with family members about your goals and the support you need, or creating a dedicated workspace that helps you maintain focus.

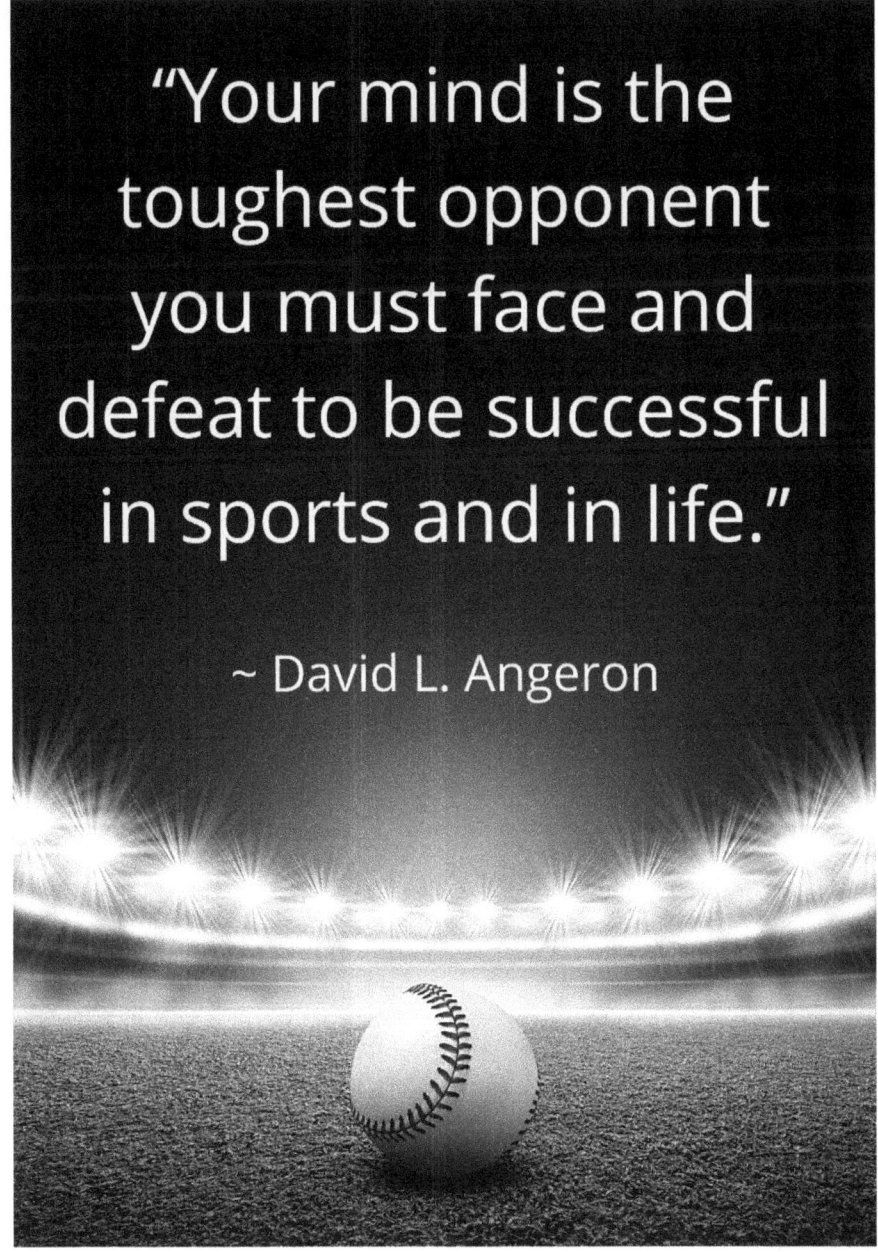

"Your mind is the toughest opponent you must face and defeat to be successful in sports and in life." - David L. Angeron

This quote underscores the importance of mental strength in achieving success. Overcoming mental barriers often proves more challenging than physical ones, making mental training a crucial component of your overall development.

For Coaches and Supervisors: When team members lose motivation or direction, engage them. Ask why they're there and what drives them. Help create simple, achievable goals based on their performance. Your attention alone can reignite their passion. Regular one-on-one meetings and personalized goal-setting can significantly boost team morale and productivity.

For Parents: Instill responsibility in your children through household and yard work. This can foster a sense of duty that translates to their team commitments. By assigning age-appropriate tasks and explaining their importance, you can help your children develop a strong work ethic from an early age.

Embrace These Powerful Motivational Tips:

1. Act when feeling low: Learn to push through lethargy. Trick your mind into action. This could involve starting with small, manageable tasks to build momentum.
2. Champions are self-made: Ignore flattery. True champions know greatness comes from relentless self-improvement, not innate talent. Cultivate a growth mindset that values effort and learning over natural ability.
3. Choose motivation daily: Create vision boards featuring your next opponent or current goal. Make motivation a

conscious, daily decision. This could involve setting daily affirmations or reviewing your goals each morning.
4. Make every day count: Set long-term goals, but commit 100% to today's objectives. Break down larger goals into daily actionable steps to maintain focus and progress.
5. Focus on the present: Remember that winning is a byproduct of moment-to-moment excellence. Stay mindful and give your full attention to the task at hand, rather than worrying about future outcomes.

You have the power to absorb and embody a strong work ethic. But is your heart truly ready for the next level? Are your core values aligned with ethical principles? Have you explored the wisdom of The Holy Bible, where work is exalted as a virtuous activity demanding commitment to excellence?

The Challenging Road to Success

The Bible implores us to work heartily and unto the Lord - to prioritize the greater good over individual gain. By putting team goals first, you'll foster a sense of unity and belonging, crucial when facing formidable opponents. This principle applies equally in sports, business, and life, emphasizing the importance of collaboration and shared purpose.

Biblical ethics can be distilled into three powerful categories:

1. Command: The Book of Proverbs extols hard work and warns against idleness (NIV, Proverb 6:6). Manual labor is noble - even kings work with their hands (ESV, 1 Samuel 11:5), and Jesus himself was an artisan (ESV, Mark 6:3). Ecclesiastes 9:10 (ESV) commands, "Whatever your hand finds to do, do it with all your might." A strong work ethic isn't just suggested - it's mandated. These biblical teachings underscore the inherent value of work and the importance of giving our best effort in all endeavors.

2. Consequences: Consider the greater good in your actions. Leviticus 23:22 (NRSV) instructs, "When you reap the harvest of your land, do not reap to the very edges of your field or gather the gleanings of your harvest. Leave them for the poor and the aliens. I am the Lord your God." This embodies the principle of utilitarianism - the greatest good for the greatest number.

It teaches us to consider the wider impact of our actions and to use our success to benefit others.

3. Character: Recognize that your actions ripple beyond yourself. You're part of a community that shapes and is shaped by your conduct. Proverbs 6:6-11 (NIV) challenges us: "Go to the ant, you sluggard; consider its ways and be wise! It has no commander, no overseer or ruler, yet it stores its provisions in summer and gathers its food at harvest. How long will you lie there, you sluggard? When will you get up from your sleep?" This passage emphasizes the importance of self-motivation and diligence, qualities that are crucial in developing a strong work ethic.

Embrace these principles, and watch as your work ethic transforms not just your performance, but your entire life. The path to greatness lies before you - will you have the courage and commitment to walk it? Remember, developing a strong work ethic is not a one-time decision, but a daily choice to push yourself towards excellence. By consistently applying these principles in your sports career, business endeavors, and personal life, you'll not only achieve greater success but also become a positive influence on those around you.

PERFORMANCE JOURNAL

Chapter 10

SETTING SMARTER GOALS: YOUR PATH TO EXCELLENCE

Embark on a transformative journey through this chapter, designed to enrich your life and propel you towards greatness. We'll explore three essential dimensions of goal-setting:

1. Theoretical Foundation: Discover the immense power of SMARTER GOALS in unleashing your full potential as an athlete or performer.
2. Psychological Mastery: Learn to craft a bulletproof plan and develop the mental fortitude needed to elevate your performance from good to extraordinary.
3. Spiritual Alignment: Uncover the profound wisdom in aligning your goals with a higher purpose, ensuring resilience when faced with unexpected challenges.

Let's dive into the heart of achievement - the goal. What's the most fundamental element in your journey to becoming an Elite Athlete? It's setting an achievable, yet ambitious goal. But here's the crucial distinction: it's not just about what you get by achieving your goal, it's about who you become in the process.

Imagine your path to success as an intricate dance. Every step matters. Your goals are the choreography guiding your movements, giving you purpose and direction. They ignite your motivation, build unwavering self-confidence, and propel you past inevitable slumps. I challenge you to dream big, then break those dreams into manageable, actionable steps.

Without goals, you're playing a game without a scoreboard. You can't gauge your progress, and the lack of purpose will eventually lead to boredom and abandonment. But with clear, compelling goals, you'll find yourself eager to leap out of bed each morning, ready to conquer new challenges.

Why focus on small steps towards SMARTER GOALS? Because these incremental achievements are measurable, tangible proof of your progress. They fuel positivity and persistence, constantly pushing you to new heights. With each step, you're not just inching closer to your dream - you're becoming the person capable of achieving it.

Life may occasionally derail your plans, perhaps through injury or unexpected setbacks. Remember, flexibility is strength. Adjust your goals when necessary, but never lose sight of your ultimate vision. Every goal, no matter how small, is a crucial piece of your larger success story.

Consider the inspiring example of Hall of Famer Carl Yastrzemski. He embraced the grind of off-season preparation, not for immediate gratification, but to forge unbreakable mental toughness. "I hated to do weights. I hated to run. But I did them," he said. "I swung a lead bat and hit balls - 300 to 400 a day - into a net for one reason: to toughen myself mentally."

This mental fortitude is your secret weapon. Train your mind, and your body will follow. Imagine the exhilaration of conquering those 75 morning push-ups, fueled by your ironclad mindset. Incorporate meditation into your routine - just 20 minutes, three times a week - to sharpen your focus on the process, not just the outcomes.

Now, let's unlock the power of SMARTER goals:

The Challenging Road to Success

Specific, Measurable, Action-oriented, Realistic, Time-bound, Evaluated, and Rewarding.

Be Specific: Clarity is power. Ask yourself:

- What precise steps will lead to your goal?
- What exactly do you aim to accomplish?
- When will you achieve this goal?
- Why is this goal vital to you?

Make it Measurable: Quantify your progress:

- What specific actions will you take tomorrow?
- How will you know you've reached your goal?
- What key indicators will track your progress?

Take Action: Define the concrete steps that will propel you towards your goal.

Stay Realistic: Challenge yourself, but remain grounded. Is your goal achievable with your current resources and commitment level?

Set a Timeline: Deadlines create urgency. When precisely will you reach your goal?

Evaluate Consistently: Partner with two trusted allies to share your goals. Their support will keep you accountable and motivated.

Reward Your Progress: Celebrate not just what you achieve, but who you become. Which is more valuable - the trophy, or the champion you've transformed into?

Now, let's delve deeper into the psychological aspect of goal achievement. Do you have the mental resilience to see your measurable goals through to completion? At Mental Master

Training, our mission is to empower athletes, performers, business professionals, and parents to fulfill their goals and unlock their full potential.

Your plan is set. You've established challenging goals, committed to regular feedback, and maintained a bird's-eye view of your progress. But what about the mental fortitude required to persevere through the countless small steps? What will fuel your motivation when the journey gets tough?

Understanding the human mind is crucial. While some theories view humans as passive and driven by psychological needs, we embrace the cognitive theory. This perspective sees humans as active initiators, driven by their interpretation of achievement. Your achievements hold personal and social value, giving deeper meaning to your journey.

Embrace a task orientation in your mental training. This approach enhances learning, fosters a commitment to society, and reduces anxiety. You'll find your information processing improving, your intuition sharpening, and your overall well-being flourishing. Most importantly, your journey will find harmony - each step perfectly choreographed towards your ultimate goal.

But what if you stumble? What if factors beyond your control lead to a setback? This is where faith and a higher purpose become your unshakeable foundation.

God's Plan: Your Ultimate Safety Net

When worldly goals fall short, remember that you're part of a greater design. As stated in Jeremiah 29:11 (AMPC), "For I know the thoughts and plans that I have for you, says the Lord, thoughts and plans for welfare and peace and not for evil, to give you hope in your final outcome."

God brings balance to your life, placing you at the center of His creation. He's made you an integral part of His plan, never abandoning you. When setting goals, seek His will. Ask for guidance and remain attentive to His answers. Often, we make plans based on ego without consulting God, then turn to Him only when those plans crumble. Why not include Him from the start?

Even if a God-inspired plan seems to fail, trust that He has something even greater in store for you. Have faith in His process.

A relationship with God as your ultimate teammate will bring more success and satisfaction than any material achievement ever could.

Proverbs 3:5-6 (NIV) reminds us: "Trust in the Lord with all your heart and lean not on your own understanding; in all your ways submit to him, and he will make your paths straight."

Recognize that you're part of something infinite and certain, a gift you've received freely. Let this realization reignite your belief and motivation. Now, armed with the power of SMARTER Goals, a rock-solid plan, and unwavering faith, you're ready to become the best athlete, performer, or business professional you can be.

Chapter Highlights:

- ♦ Embrace SMARTER goals: Specific, Measurable, Action-oriented, Realistic, Time-bound, Evaluated, and Rewarding.
- ♦ Adopt a master approach, striving for goals with broader social impact rather than ego-driven achievements.
- ♦ Align your goals with a higher purpose, finding strength and guidance in faith when faced with challenges.

Your journey to greatness starts now. Set your SMARTER Goals, craft your plan, and relentlessly pursue excellence in every aspect of your life.

Setting SMARTER Goals: Your Path to Excellence

Chapter Work-Up: Crafting Your Path to Success

Embark on a transformative journey of goal-setting that will propel you towards your dreams. This powerful exercise is designed to ignite your imagination and translate your aspirations into actionable plans. Whether you're aiming for personal growth or athletic excellence, this process will help you chart a clear course to success.

Unleash Your Dreams

1. I've always wanted to _____

2. It would be exhilarating to _____

3. This may seem audacious, but I'm determined to _____

4. I've been told I have a natural talent for _____, and I'm excited to explore this potential.

Now, let's transform these dreams into concrete, achievable goals.

Ambitious Long-Term Goals

1. By (target date) _____, I will accomplish (state your dream) _____

I'll celebrate achieving this goal when: _____

Am I fully committed to this goal? _____

Key steps to reach this goal: _____

My first action towards this goal tomorrow: _____

2. By (target date) _____, I will achieve (state your dream) _____

I'll know I've succeeded when: _____

My level of commitment to this goal: _____

Crucial steps to attain this goal: _____

Immediate action I'll take tomorrow: _____

Strategic Short-Term Goals

Break down your long-term goals into manageable milestones:

1. By (near-future date) _____, I will accomplish _____

Success indicator for this goal: _____

My dedication to this goal: _____

Essential steps to achieve this: _____

Action I'll take tomorrow: _____

2. By (near-future date) _____, I will achieve _____

How I'll measure success: _____

My commitment level: _____

Key actions for this goal: _____

What I'll do tomorrow: _____

3. By (near-future date) _____, I will reach _____

Tangible proof of achievement: _____

My resolve to accomplish this: _____

Critical steps to success: _____

My immediate action plan: _____

Inspiring Example: From Dream to Reality

Dream: Conquer a marathon

Long-term goal: By next May, I will triumphantly cross the finish line of our local marathon.

- Success looks like: Sprinting through the finish line, proudly displaying my runner's number as a symbol of my achievement.
- Commitment level: Absolutely. I'm driven to outperform my friend's time and prove to myself I can conquer this challenge.
- Key steps: Develop a rigorous training regimen, cultivate unwavering motivation, and optimize my nutrition for peak performance.
- Tomorrow's action: Invest in top-quality running shoes and embark on my first training run, officially launching my journey to marathon success.

Short-term goal: Adhere religiously to my six-month training schedule.

- Measure of success: Daily log of distances covered and times achieved, visually tracking my progress on my calendar.

- Commitment: Unwavering. I'm determined to cross that finish line strong, avoiding injury and surpassing my own expectations.
- Critical steps: Seamlessly integrate training into my work schedule, rally support from my inner circle, and prioritize my marathon goal over less important activities.
- Tomorrow's plan: Increase my water intake, overhaul my diet with a strategic grocery run, and complete my first scheduled training run, setting the tone for the months ahead.

Remember, every step you take brings you closer to your dreams. Embrace this journey of self-discovery and achievement. Your potential is limitless - now go out there and make it happen!

PERFORMANCE JOURNAL

Chapter 11
WHO AM I? RECOGNIZING PERSONALITY TYPES

This groundbreaking chapter isn't merely about educating you—it's about catalyzing a profound transformation, molding you into the optimal version of yourself. We're not simply engineering a high-performance machine; we're cultivating a well-rounded individual poised for success across the multifaceted landscapes of sports, business, and life. The journey ahead promises to be both challenging and rewarding, pushing you beyond your perceived limitations and unlocking potential you may not have realized existed within you.

Prepare to embark on an illuminating odyssey of self-discovery and personal growth as we delve deep into three crucial, interconnected aspects of personal development. These pillars form the foundation upon which we'll build your path to excellence:

1. Theoretical Insight: Uncover the intricate depths of an athlete's personality and explore how these unique characteristics shape performance, both on and off the field. We'll examine cutting-edge research in sports psychology and personality theory to provide you with a comprehensive understanding of the complex interplay between individual traits and athletic achievement.
2. Psychological Wisdom: Harness the transformative power of emotional intelligence and embrace the timeless golden rule of interpersonal relationships. Learn to navigate the subtle nuances of human interaction, developing the empathy and self-awareness necessary to excel in team environments and leadership roles.
3. Spiritual Enlightenment: Explore the profound, far-reaching impact of loving your neighbor and its myriad benefits, not just in your personal life, but in your professional and athletic endeavors as well. Discover how cultivating a spirit of compassion and understanding can elevate your performance and enrich your overall life experience.

Drawing from my acclaimed work, "The Mental Training Guide for Elite Athletes," we'll elevate your understanding of personal growth to unprecedented heights. Having mastered the art of setting "smarter goals," gained a deeper comprehension of your place in the world, and honed your skills in crafting achievable plans, it's time to push your boundaries even further. This chapter serves as a bridge, connecting the foundational knowledge you've acquired to the advanced concepts that will propel you towards true mastery.

As the ancient Greek philosopher Socrates wisely proclaimed, "To know thyself is the beginning of wisdom." This timeless adage serves as our guiding principle as we embark on this journey of self-discovery. Embrace your uniqueness, recognize your distinctive attitude, and acknowledge your individual character. Don't simply mimic your favorite athlete's technique or emulate a successful business leader's strategies—discover your own path to greatness.

The Challenging Road to Success

This heightened self-awareness will serve as a catapult, propelling you into the upper echelons of success in your chosen field.

Extraversion: The Outgoing Dynamo

Extraverts thrive on engagement with the external world, drawing energy and inspiration from their surroundings and interactions with others. These sociable, energetic, and action-oriented individuals crave the spotlight and eagerly embrace new experiences, viewing challenges as exciting opportunities rather than daunting obstacles. Their natural enthusiasm can be a powerful asset, infusing teams with positivity and driving projects forward with unparalleled momentum. However, it's crucial to channel this vibrant energy responsibly, ensuring that it enhances rather than disrupts team dynamics. Remember: respect for your sport or profession is paramount, and unbridled enthusiasm must always be tempered with consideration for others and adherence to established norms and expectations.

On the flip side of the personality spectrum, we find introverts—individuals who carefully consider their thoughts before speaking, often preferring to process information internally before sharing their insights. These contemplative souls focus intensely on their own performance rather than seeking external validation or attention. It's important to note that introversion is far from being antisocial; instead, introverts simply prefer quiet reflection and derive their energy from solitude or small-group interactions. Their capacity for deep, independent thinking can be a tremendous asset to any team, offering thoughtful perspectives and well-considered solutions that may be overlooked in more boisterous environments.

Are you an extravert? Look for these telltale signs:

- You eagerly share ideas and speak up in group settings, often being the first to break the ice or offer suggestions in meetings or team huddles.
- You naturally take charge and relish leadership opportunities, feeling energized by the prospect of guiding others towards a common goal.
- You feel invigorated by social interaction and tend to avoid prolonged solitude, seeking out company and collaborative activities whenever possible.
- You think out loud, processing your thoughts through verbal expression and dialogue with others.
- You have a wide circle of friends and acquaintances, and you enjoy meeting new people and expanding your network.

Or do you lean towards introversion?

- You prefer to listen and observe in group settings, taking time to process information before contributing your thoughts.
- You recharge by spending time alone after social engagements, finding solitude necessary for maintaining your energy and focus.

The Challenging Road to Success

- ♦ You're content to let others take the lead in group situations, offering support and insights from a more reserved position.
- ♦ You carefully guard your thoughts and opinions, sharing them selectively with those you trust most.
- ♦ You prefer deep, meaningful conversations with a small group of close friends over large social gatherings or networking events.
- ♦ You excel in tasks that require concentration and independent work, finding satisfaction in solitary pursuits.

Tailored Strategies for Success:

Introverts: Challenge yourself to share your valuable insights with your team more frequently. Your unique perspective is invaluable, and your teammates can benefit greatly from your thoughtful contributions. Take the initiative to discuss ideas with your coach or supervisor in one-on-one settings where you feel more comfortable. Set a goal to lead in your unique, thoughtful way—perhaps by spearheading a project that aligns with your strengths or mentoring a younger team member. Immerse yourself in literature about introverts thriving in sports and business—let their stories inspire you and provide practical strategies for leveraging your introversion as a strength.

Extraverts: Cultivate self-reflection as a counterbalance to your natural outward focus. Regularly ask yourself, "How will my ideas impact others?" before sharing them in group settings. Consider the needs and perspectives of those around you, particularly your more introverted teammates who may require time to process and respond. Actively seek out and genuinely listen to others' opinions, practicing the art of active listening to enhance your interpersonal skills. Embrace moments of solitude to focus on personal growth and goal-setting, using this time for introspection and strategic planning.

The Challenging Road to Success

INTROVERT

EXTROVERT

Coaches and Supervisors: Tailor your approach to each personality type to maximize individual and team performance. For introverts, avoid confrontational tactics or putting them on the spot in large group settings. Instead, offer logical solutions and constructive criticism in a supportive, one-on-one environment. Introverts thrive on sincere, well-earned praise, so be sure to recognize their contributions, even if they're not the most vocal team members. For extraverts, provide clear, energetic feedback in group settings where they can engage in dynamic discussion. Follow up with positive reinforcement after performances to fuel their natural enthusiasm. Channel their outgoing nature towards productive goals, such as team building or client relations, where their social skills can shine.

Neuroticism: Navigating Emotional Landscapes

Neuroticism reflects an individual's emotional stability and tendency to experience negative emotions. Those with low neuroticism tend to be even-tempered and resilient, maintaining composure under pressure and bouncing back quickly from setbacks. On the other hand, individuals higher on the neuroticism scale may experience more frequent mood fluctuations and emotional intensity. Neurotic personalities often have lower stress tolerance and may react impulsively to challenging situations. It's crucial to remember that we're all human, with our own unique emotional tendencies—your power lies in understanding and working with your natural inclinations rather than against them.

Identifying Your Emotional Type:

Stable/Conscientious:

- ♦ You're agreeable, coachable, and work well with diverse personalities, adapting easily to different team dynamics.
- ♦ You prefer group consensus to quick, individual decisions, valuing collaboration and harmony in decision-making processes.
- ♦ You maintain emotional equilibrium in high-pressure situations, serving as a stabilizing force for your team.
- ♦ You approach challenges with a calm, methodical attitude, breaking down complex problems into manageable steps.

Wired/Neurotic:

- ♦ You experience frequent anxiety and act on impulse, sometimes making decisions based on emotional reactions rather than logical analysis.
- ♦ You often feel stressed and arrive early to events out of nervous energy, using preparation as a coping mechanism for anxiety.
- ♦ You're highly sensitive to criticism and may struggle with self-doubt, requiring more frequent reassurance and support.
- ♦ You experience emotions intensely, which can fuel your passion and drive but may also lead to burnout if not managed effectively.

Strategies for Growth:

Stable/Conscientious: Assert yourself more frequently in team settings. While your agreeable nature is an asset, it's important to share opinions that may challenge the status quo when necessary. This can lead to innovative solutions and personal growth. Prioritize your individual needs as an athlete or professional, ensuring that your desire for harmony doesn't come at the expense of your own development. Set personal goals that push you slightly out of your comfort zone, embracing calculated risks that can lead to significant improvements in your performance.

Wired/Neurotic: Focus on achieving balance in your performance by developing coping strategies for stress and anxiety. Embrace change through relaxation techniques and meditation, incorporating these practices into your daily routine to build emotional resilience. Listen actively to others' perspectives, using their input as a way to broaden your viewpoint and reduce overthinking. Develop a structured pre-performance routine that helps channel nervous energy productively. Work with a mental health professional or sports psychologist to develop personalized strategies for managing your emotional intensity and leveraging it as a strength rather than a hindrance.

Coaches and Supervisors: Guide conscientious athletes with clear direction, encouraging independent decision-making and maintaining motivation through consistent, positive reinforcement. Create opportunities for these individuals to step into leadership roles, helping them develop assertiveness in a supportive environment. For neurotic individuals, implement daily relaxation routines to manage anxiety, such as guided meditation or progressive muscle relaxation. Establish consistent pre-game rituals to prevent last-minute stress, providing a sense of control and predictability. Offer frequent, constructive feedback to address their need for reassurance, while also helping them develop internal validation mechanisms.

Emotional Intelligence: The Key to Harmony

Developing emotional intelligence is crucial for creating harmony in your life and team dynamics. It embodies the wisdom behind the age-old adage, "Treat others as you want to be treated," applying this principle to the nuanced world of emotions and interpersonal relationships. Emotional intelligence allows you to identify and manage your own emotions effectively while empathizing with others, creating a bridge of understanding that transcends personal differences. This invaluable skill enhances interpersonal relationships, facilitates conflict resolution, and is a hallmark of great leaders and team players across all fields.

By honing your emotional intelligence, you'll become more aware of your emotional states—from intense frustration to subtle mood shifts—and learn to manage them effectively. This self-awareness is the foundation upon which you can build better self-regulation, allowing you to respond thoughtfully to challenges rather than reacting impulsively. Simultaneously, you'll develop a keen sense of others' emotions, fostering stronger connections in all areas of life, from personal relationships to professional collaborations.

As an athlete or professional, learn to "read" your teammates and colleagues. Observe facial expressions, body language, and energy levels with the same intensity you apply to your sport or work. These non-verbal indicators provide crucial insights into emotional states, allowing you to respond with empathy and support. By attuning yourself to these subtle cues, you'll be better equipped to motivate, console, or celebrate with your peers, strengthening team cohesion and improving overall performance.

The Power of "Love Thy Neighbor"

Extending emotional intelligence beyond your immediate circle to your broader community is vital for holistic success. Your neighborhood—whether it's your local community, your professional network, or the global community of your sport—is a microcosm of the world. Living in harmony with this extended "neighborhood" is not just natural, it's essential for your growth and well-being. This principle encourages you to view success not as a zero-sum game, but as a collaborative effort that uplifts all involved.

Remember, focusing solely on self-love can lead to dissatisfaction and self-deception. While self-care is important, true fulfillment comes from balancing it with genuine care for others. As the scripture reminds us, "Love thy neighbor as thyself" is a fundamental principle for a life well-lived. This balanced approach fosters a sense of connection and purpose that transcends individual achievement, leading to more sustainable and meaningful success.

By embracing these principles of self-awareness, emotional intelligence, and community engagement, you'll not only excel in your chosen field but also become a beacon of positive influence in the world around you. This holistic approach to personal development ensures that your success is not just measured in trophies or accolades, but in the lives you touch and the positive change you inspire in your community and beyond.

PERFORMANCE JOURNAL

Chapter 12
FORGING MENTAL AND PHYSICAL TOUGHNESS

What is pain? Why does it feel unbearable? How can you endure it? These profound questions strike at the very core of mental and physical toughness - essential qualities for any athlete, leader, or high achiever in today's competitive world. Understanding and mastering these concepts can be the difference between mediocrity and excellence, between giving up and pushing through to victory.

Pain is an inevitable part of life, especially in an athlete's journey. However, when harnessed correctly, it can become a powerful catalyst propelling you forward. The key lies in developing the mental resilience to not just tolerate pain, but to embrace it as a tool for growth. Mental toughness, often defined as the ability to consistently perform towards the upper range of your talent and skill regardless of circumstances, is the critical component that separates the good from the great. It's the quality that allows individuals to bounce back from adversity, to maintain focus under pressure, and to persevere when others might falter.

Without mental toughness, even the most promising talents can see their growth stunted. History is replete with examples of gifted individuals who failed to reach their potential due to a lack of mental fortitude. Conversely, there are numerous instances of athletes and leaders who, through sheer determination and mental strength, have overcome seemingly insurmountable odds to achieve greatness.

Parents, in your quest to support your young athletes, resist the urge to coddle them excessively. While it's natural to want to protect and nurture your children, overprotection can inadvertently hinder their development of crucial life skills. Instead of carrying their equipment while they engage with their smartphones, empower them with manageable tasks that build character. Let them haul their own gear, manage their own schedules, and face minor challenges head-on. This approach lays the foundation for a strong work ethic and self-discipline - qualities that will serve them well not just in sports, but in all aspects of life.

In the world of sports, most minor injuries fall under what we call the "30-Second Rule." This principle suggests that the pain from these minor setbacks typically subsides within half a minute, allowing the athlete to move on and continue performing. The old adage of "rub some dirt on it and get back in the game" might sound harsh, but it encapsulates a valuable lesson in resilience. Of course, for serious injuries, it's crucial to trust the judgment of medical professionals. But for everything else, cultivating resilience is key.

Adult performers, whether in sports, business, or any other field, must guard vigilantly against negative self-talk during setbacks. While you can't control external factors like injuries or unexpected challenges, you have complete mastery over your mind. It's essential to recognize that your comeback begins in your thoughts. Renew your principles and beliefs regularly, reinforcing your mental fortitude. Remember, it's not the adversity itself that defines you, but how you respond to it.

The 4 Cs of Mental Toughness

Dr. Peter Clough, a pioneering researcher in the field of mental toughness, developed the groundbreaking MTQ48 survey. This comprehensive assessment measures mental toughness across four critical dimensions, known as the 4 Cs. Understanding and developing these aspects can significantly enhance your mental resilience:

The Challenging Road to Success

1. Challenge: Embrace difficulties as opportunities for growth rather than threats. This mindset shift is crucial for continuous improvement. Start small - make your bed every morning, complete short-term goals, gradually increasing the complexity of challenges you take on. Remember, every habit, no matter how small, is reinforced through consistent action. By regularly facing and overcoming challenges, you build the mental muscle to tackle larger obstacles in the future.

2. Commitment: Honor your word, both to yourself and to others. This goes beyond mere promise-keeping; it's about developing a deep-seated sense of responsibility and dedication. If you commit to running four miles, follow through, regardless of how you feel in the moment. Excellence demands consistent effort, and commitment is the glue that holds your efforts together over time. By consistently honoring your commitments, you build trust in yourself and from others, creating a solid foundation for success.

3. Control: While you may not have power over your environment or external circumstances, you always have control over your reaction. This dimension of mental toughness is about maintaining composure and adapting your plans in the face of disruption. It involves managing your emotions effectively, staying focused on your goals, and finding alternative paths when obstacles arise. Developing a strong sense of control allows you to remain

calm and make rational decisions even in high-pressure situations.

4. Confidence: Cultivate an unwavering belief in your ability to overcome adversity and achieve your goals. This isn't about baseless optimism, but a deep-seated faith in your skills, preparation, and resilience. Stand firm against unexpected challenges, drawing strength from your past successes and the knowledge that you've prepared thoroughly. Confidence is both a result of and a contributor to mental toughness, creating a positive feedback loop that enhances performance.

Your response to pressure defines your performance. In high-stakes situations, mental toughness can be the deciding factor between success and failure. Preparation is key to developing this crucial quality. By incorporating the following daily habits into your routine, you can systematically build both mental and physical toughness:

- Begin each day with a powerful, personalized mantra. For example: "I am ready for any challenge that comes my way. I am fully committed to my work and my team. I am in control of my reactions and emotions. What stands in my way becomes the way forward." Repeat this mantra with conviction, allowing it to set the tone for your day.

- Plan meticulously to honor your commitments. This might mean waking up earlier to fit in your training sessions or rearranging your schedule to meet your responsibilities. By consistently following through on your commitments, you reinforce your mental toughness and build a reputation for reliability.

- Take immediate control of negative self-talk. When you catch yourself engaging in pessimistic or self-defeating thoughts, consciously redirect your mental energy to productive action. Replace "I can't do this" with "This is challenging, but I'm capable of finding a solution."

- Build confidence through consistent effort and gradual progress. Set ambitious yet achievable goals and work relentlessly towards them. Remember, if you fall short, let it be in the attempt, not for lack of trying. Each small victory builds your confidence and prepares you for greater challenges.

It's crucial to understand that mental strength isn't an innate, fixed trait - it's a skill that can be developed and honed over time. Just as you train your body for physical performance, you must also train your mind for mental resilience. Your body ultimately follows where your mind leads, which is why elite athletes prioritize mental training alongside physical conditioning. They focus on cultivating grit - the passion and perseverance for long-term goals - recognizing it as a key factor in sustained success.

The great civil rights leader, Martin Luther King, Jr., eloquently captured the essence of mental toughness when he said, "The ultimate measure of a man is not where he stands in moments of comfort and convenience, but where he stands at times of challenge and controversy." Sports, much like life itself, have a unique way of revealing your true character and your will to achieve. They present a microcosm of the challenges you'll face in the broader world, testing your resilience, determination, and ability to perform under pressure. The question is: Do you have the mental toughness to not just survive, but thrive in a tough, often selfish world?

For coaches and supervisors, establishing clear ground rules for handling injuries, setbacks, and frustrations is paramount. Develop a comprehensive protocol that outlines how to respond to various challenges, ensuring consistency and fairness in your approach. Moreover, take the time to understand your team members' individual personalities and motivations. This knowledge will allow you to tailor your responses when adversity strikes, providing the right balance of support and challenge to each person.

Parents play a crucial role in developing mental toughness in young athletes. Your goal should be to act as an enabler of growth, not a crutch that hampers development. While it's important to monitor your child's emotional well-being, it's equally vital to empower them to make decisions and carry their own load. Guide them towards resilience by allowing them to face and overcome age-appropriate challenges. Don't shield them from every difficulty; instead, teach them how to navigate obstacles effectively. This approach will equip them with the mental tools they need to succeed not just in sports, but in all areas of life.

The Challenging Road to Success

"I can do all things through him who gives me strength"
Philippians 4:13

Spiritual Strength: The Ultimate Source of Power

When you find yourself at the limits of your mental and physical capabilities, feeling weak and overwhelmed, remember this powerful truth: "I can do all things through Christ who strengthens me" (Philippians 4:13). This verse from the Bible reminds us of the limitless source of strength available to those who put their faith in God. It's a reminder that our own abilities, while important, are not the ultimate determinant of our success or failure.

The prophet Isaiah offers further encouragement in Isaiah 40:31, affirming, "But those who hope in the LORD will renew their strength. They will soar on wings like eagles; they will run and not grow weary, they will walk and not be faint." This beautiful imagery illustrates the supernatural endurance and resilience available to those who place their trust in God. It suggests that spiritual strength can transcend physical limitations, allowing us to persevere even when our bodies and minds feel ready to give up.

In the New Testament, we find a call to mental and spiritual transformation. Romans 12:2 urges believers, "Do not conform to the pattern of this world, but be transformed by the renewing of your mind." This passage emphasizes the importance of our thought patterns in shaping our actions and character. By aligning our thinking with God's truth, we can develop a mindset that is resilient, positive, and focused on what truly matters.

The apostle Paul, writing to his protégé Timothy, reminds us that God has equipped us with inner resources to face life's challenges. In 2 Timothy 1:7, he states, "For God has not given us a spirit of fear, but of power and of love and of a sound mind." This verse encapsulates the essence of mental toughness from a spiritual perspective - power to act, love to motivate, and a sound mind to make wise decisions under pressure.

Mental toughness, viewed through a spiritual lens, requires belief, and belief requires faith. However, this faith is not meant to be passive. We are called to actively engage with our spiritual resources. As Ephesians 3:16 encourages, we should pray to "be strengthened with power through his Spirit in your inner being." This active approach to spiritual strength aligns perfectly with the proactive stance required for developing mental toughness in all areas of life.

It's crucial to remember that you're not alone in this journey of developing mental and spiritual toughness. The wisdom literature of the Bible, specifically Ecclesiastes 4:9-13, reminds us of the power of community: "Two are better than one, because they have a good return for their labor: If either of them falls down, one can help the other up. But pity anyone who falls and has no one to help them up... A cord of three strands is not quickly broken." This passage underscores the importance of supportive relationships in building resilience.

As you face challenges in sports, business, or life, remember to lean on your teammates, draw strength from your faith community, and face every obstacle with renewed determination. The power within you - a combination of your innate abilities, developed skills, mental toughness, and spiritual strength - is greater than any challenge you may face. You have the capacity to overcome, to excel, and to lead. Whether on the sports field, in the boardroom, or in your personal life, tap into this wellspring of strength. Let it propel you towards your goals, help you bounce back from setbacks, and enable you to inspire others along the way.

The Challenging Road to Success

PERFORMANCE JOURNAL

Chapter 13
Living in the Present - Carpe Diem

Imagine the power of a single moment. Indestructible. Unborn. Transmitted. Inherited. Flowing eternally on time's continuum. Everything - absolutely everything - happens within this precious instant. It's your only true access point to reality. Why is this crucial? Why does it hold the key to your success? This chapter will reveal how living in the present keeps you acutely aware, deeply connected, and firmly grounded in your journey towards excellence.

Embracing the present is a rigorous demand, but one that yields immeasurable rewards. As the great Stoic philosopher Seneca urgently advises, "Even though you seize the day, it still will flee; therefore, you must vie with time's swiftness in the speed of using it, and, as from a torrent that rushes by and will not always flow, you must drink quickly." This profound statement underscores the fleeting nature of time and the importance of making every moment

The Challenging Road to Success

count. In our modern world, distractions vie relentlessly for your attention - advertisements, social media notifications, endless streams of information - all competing for your precious time. The solution? A conscious choice. Your deliberate decision to focus on the present moment is what puts you at the epicenter of your own success story.

Marcus Aurelius, in his timeless "Meditations," implores us to let no action be without purpose. This ancient wisdom remains remarkably relevant in our fast-paced, often chaotic world. As a high-performer, what's your purpose? Are you competing for it with every fiber of your being? Are you competing in the now? This chapter will guide you towards developing a self-reliant mind, empowering you to stand firm amidst life's chaos. As Ralph Waldo Emerson eloquently states, "The great man is he who in the midst of the crowd keeps with perfect sweetness the independence of solitude." True performers never waver from their aim, constantly honing themselves in moments of solitude. How can you attain this state? By being acutely aware of the present.

Take inspiration from Alex Rodriguez's powerful words: "Winners live in the present tense. People who come up short are consumed with the future or past. I want to be living in the now." This isn't just motivational speak - it's a proven strategy for success. Having coached hundreds of professional athletes and consulted numerous successful business professionals, I can assure you: the information you're about to receive is pure, distilled knowledge. And true to the essence of this series, we'll also nourish your spirit along the way, providing a holistic approach to personal and professional growth.

Picture yourself in the heat of competition. Can you visualize tracking the ball's movement with laser-like focus? Nothing else matters - no past failures, no future anxieties - just you and the ball.

This is the essence of <u>competing in the now</u>. This state of intense focus and presence is what separates elite performers from the rest.

This vital skill sharpens your mental awareness and laser-focuses your performance. When doubt creeps in, you've allowed negative emotions to overwhelm you. Anger, fear, and anguish don't lurk outside - they reside in your heart and mind. These emotions, whether stemming from past regrets or future worries, delay your response, cloud your judgment, and prevent peak performance. Your goal? Get your mind firmly rooted in the present moment. Here, everything slows down, clarity emerges, and you regain control. It's about honoring the now. In this state, struggle dissolves, and your performance flows with joy and ease.

Let's make this concept concrete with a powerful example. Imagine a running back who fumbles, leading to an easy touchdown for the opposing team. Devastated, he replays the scene endlessly. "How could I have done that? I should have... I could have..." Then, future worries flood in. "What if we lose because of me? I've let the whole team down!" This spiral of negative thinking only magnifies emotional distress and creates immense pressure, often leading to more errors. The player's mind is trapped between past regrets and future anxieties, completely disconnected from the present moment where their performance is most needed.

But there's hope. You can break this cycle and reclaim your power in the present moment. Here are four potent mantras to use when you feel yourself drifting from your immediate self:

1. Take a Deep Breath: Your breath is your anchor to the now. Breathe deeply into your belly, feeling the connection between mind and body. Let thoughts flow without judgment, then release them. This simple act of conscious breathing can instantly bring you back to the present moment, calming your nerves and clearing your mind.
2. Use Your Senses: Engage all five senses to ground yourself in the present. Feel the baseball's seams, taste the sweat and adrenaline, hear the crowd's roar. Bring every sensation into your consciousness, allowing your emotions to neutralize. This sensory awareness technique can help you become fully immersed in the current moment, shutting out distractions and enhancing your focus.
3. Listen to Your Self-Talk: As Marcus Aurelius wisely noted, "Very little is needed to make a happy life; it's all within yourself, in your way of thinking." Practice mindful awareness of your inner voice. Is it positive or negative? Calm or agitated? Use this awareness to cultivate purposeful, empowering self-talk. By consciously shaping your internal dialogue, you can significantly influence your emotional state and performance.
4. Fake It 'Til You Make It: Embody your best self. Visualize achieving your goals in vivid detail. Create a "reset word" to instantly refocus your mind. Remember, it's years of mental training that separate the good from the truly great. This technique of mental rehearsal and positive visualization can

help you build confidence and improve performance over time.

For Coaches and Supervisors: Ensure your performers know their roles inside and out. Train them in mindfulness and emotional neutrality. Help them identify their 'essential nature' and coach accordingly. Teach them to transform, not deny, negative emotions. Work with each individual to create personalized "reset words" and focal points. By incorporating these practices into your coaching strategy, you can help your team members develop stronger mental resilience and improve their ability to perform under pressure.

For Parents: Help your child savor moments of success without self-consciousness. Use exercises from my other book to boost competence. These techniques benefit all areas of life, reinforcing their value through daily practice. Watch as your child connects better with their surroundings, becoming not just a better performer, but a better person. By teaching children the importance of living in the present from an early age, you're equipping them with invaluable life skills that will serve them well into adulthood.

Now, let's nourish your spiritual side with the wisdom of parables. In the Parable of the Sower (Matthew 13, NIV), Jesus speaks of seeds falling on different types of soil. The seeds on good soil - those who truly hear and understand - bear abundant fruit. To be this good soil, you must develop the capacity to truly hear and live in the present moment. This parable teaches us the importance of being receptive and attentive to the wisdom and opportunities that surround us in each moment.

Jesus continually calls us to embrace the now. He warns against dwelling on the past: "No one who puts a hand to the plow and looks back is fit for service in the kingdom of God" (Luke 9:62, NIV). This powerful metaphor reminds us that focusing on past events can hinder our progress and effectiveness in the present. He also calms our future anxieties: "Therefore do not worry about tomorrow, for tomorrow will worry about itself. Each day has enough trouble of its own" (Matthew 6:34, NIV). This teaching encourages us to focus our energy on the challenges and opportunities of the present day, rather than becoming overwhelmed by future concerns.

The Challenging Road to Success

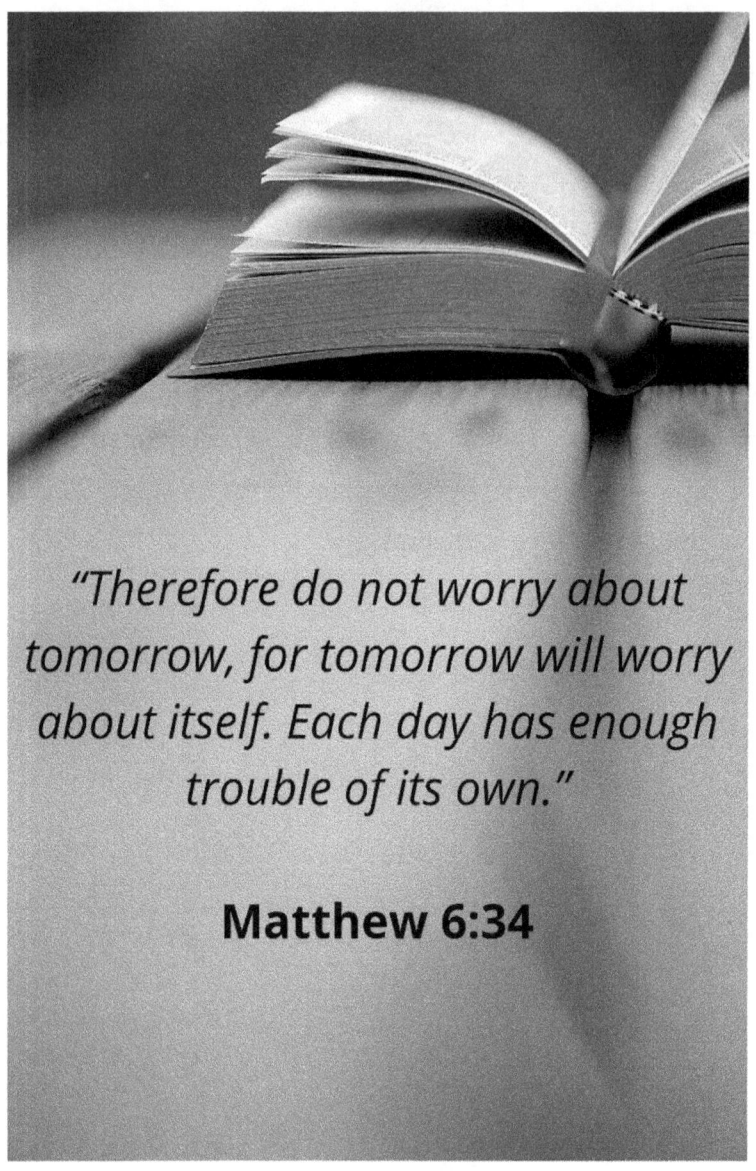

"Therefore do not worry about tomorrow, for tomorrow will worry about itself. Each day has enough trouble of its own."

Matthew 6:34

Heed these powerful words from Proverbs 27:1 (ESV): "Do not boast about tomorrow, for you do not know what a day may bring." This wisdom from the Old Testament aligns perfectly with the concept of living in the present. Echoing this, the philosopher

Seneca urges: "The whole future lies in uncertainty: Live immediately." Both of these quotes emphasize the importance of making the most of the present moment, as the future is uncertain and beyond our control. Let these words of wisdom propel you into purposeful, present-focused action.

We'll conclude with this stirring call from Ephesians 5:15-16 (ESV): "Look carefully then how you walk, not as unwise but as wise, making the best use of the time, because the days are evil." This passage encourages us to be mindful of how we live our lives, using our time wisely and purposefully. In challenging times, staying motivated and positive is crucial. Our next chapter will delve deeper into this vital topic, equipping you with even more tools for success in your journey of personal and professional growth.

PERFORMANCE JOURNAL

Chapter 14
WHAT IT REALLY TAKES TO EXCEL

Embark on an extraordinary journey through the realms of grit, determination, agility, and sports acumen. This chapter will challenge you to push your limits, both physically and mentally, as we explore the essence of what it truly takes to be a successful performer. Brace yourself for a rollercoaster ride of emotions - from the depths of hard falls to the exhilaration of spectacular rises. By the end, you'll understand why success demands not just physical prowess, but the strength of your very soul.

Throughout my professional career spanning decades in sports and leadership, I've witnessed countless physically gifted athletes who never progress beyond high school, many succumbing to burnout before they even turn 15. It's a harsh reality we must confront head-on, as it reflects not only on the world of sports but also on the broader landscape of personal and professional development. But what sets apart those who advance to college and professional sports? What propels individuals to thrive in business and life? These questions have been at the forefront of my research and experience, leading to some profound insights.

The Four Pillars of Excellence

After years of meticulous observation and hands-on experience, I've identified four critical characteristics that all successful athletes, business professionals, and high achievers share. These pillars form the foundation of excellence, regardless of the field or discipline:

1. Skills and Fundamentals: The foundation of success
2. Sports Psychology and Mental Training: The game-changer that elevates good to great
3. Knowledge of the Sport or Profession: The wisdom that guides decision-making
4. Unwavering Desire to Excel: The fire that fuels greatness

Let's delve deeper into each of these pillars and understand why they're indispensable for anyone aspiring to reach the pinnacle of their field. By thoroughly examining these elements, we can unlock the secrets to sustained success and personal fulfillment.

1. Skills and Fundamentals: Necessary, but Not Sufficient

Most high school athletes possess basic skills and invest heavily in personal training. They spend countless hours honing their speed, strength, and agility, often dedicating their summers and weekends to intensive training camps and private coaching sessions. While these attributes may make you stand out on your local field, they alone won't propel you to college or professional levels. The elite echelons demand more - much more.

Consider, for instance, the world of basketball. A high school player might excel at shooting three-pointers or executing impressive dunks. However, to compete at higher levels, they need to master complex offensive and defensive strategies, understand team dynamics, and develop the stamina to maintain peak performance throughout an entire game. Similarly, in the business world, having a particular skill set is crucial, but it's the ability to apply those skills in diverse, challenging situations that truly sets leaders apart.

2. Sports Psychology and Mental Training: The Ultimate Differentiator

This is where champions are truly forged. While physical prowess is important, mental strength is paramount. It's what separates the good from the great, the amateur from the professional. Mental training equips athletes and professionals alike to navigate the complex psychological landscape of high-performance environments.

Mental training empowers individuals to:

- ♦ Manage nerves under intense pressure, maintaining composure in critical moments

- Battle through adversity with unwavering resolve, turning challenges into opportunities
- Perform with unshakeable confidence, even when faced with formidable opponents
- Embrace failure as a stepping stone to success, learning and growing from every setback
- Bounce back from devastating injuries or career setbacks, demonstrating remarkable resilience

The mechanics of mental training are rooted in cognitive psychology - understanding how our thinking influences our responses. In the high-stakes world of sports and business, where split-second decisions can make or break careers, mental fortitude is your most valuable asset. Techniques such as visualization, positive self-talk, and mindfulness meditation have become essential tools in the arsenal of top performers across various fields.

3. Knowledge of Your Sport or Profession: The Strategic Edge

Raw talent without understanding is like a ship without a rudder - powerful but directionless. True mastery demands an intimate knowledge of your field. As a scout with years of experience evaluating talent, I've seen physically gifted players falter in critical moments due to a lack of understanding. To compete at an elite level, you must become a student of the game, constantly learning and evolving.

Having coached at every level from youth leagues to professional teams, I can attest that learning never stops. When you cease to learn, it's time to exit the game altogether. A high "Sports IQ" or "Business IQ" slows the game down, putting you in the right place at the right time. It's about understanding the nuances, anticipating moves, and making split-second decisions that can turn the tide of a game or the fortune of a company.

For instance, in baseball, it's not enough to hit the ball hard. A player with deep knowledge of the game understands pitch sequences, recognizes patterns in fielder positioning, and can adjust their strategy based on the specific situation. Similarly, in the business world, successful leaders don't just rely on their technical skills. They understand market trends, anticipate changes in consumer behavior, and make strategic decisions based on a comprehensive understanding of their industry landscape.

4. Desire: The Crowning Jewel of Success

At the apex of our pyramid of excellence sits desire - the burning passion that fuels greatness. At the highest levels, your sport or profession isn't just for fun; it's a demanding job that requires extreme work ethic, unwavering dedication, and impeccable character. This desire is what separates the truly exceptional from the merely good.

Many aspiring athletes and professionals believe they possess this desire, only to discover in college or early in their careers that they've been chasing someone else's dream. True desire comes from within - it's what gets you out of bed for early morning practices, pushes you to do one more rep when your muscles are screaming, and keeps you focused when others are distracted. It's the force that drives you to persist when others would quit, to innovate when others are content with the status quo.

This intrinsic motivation is what allows top performers to endure the grueling demands of their chosen path. It's what enables an entrepreneur to work 80-hour weeks to get their startup off the ground, or an athlete to push through painful rehabilitation after a serious injury. Without this deep-seated desire, even the most talented individuals may find themselves falling short of their potential.

The Fifth Element: Spiritual Connection

Beyond these four pillars lies a fifth element - one that's often overlooked but incredibly powerful: spiritual connection. How you connect with God, yourself, and your inner being can provide the strength and purpose needed to overcome seemingly insurmountable obstacles. This spiritual foundation can be the difference between bouncing back from setbacks and giving up entirely.

In the cutthroat world of athletics and high-stakes business, where you're always one injury or one failed project away from being replaced, finding value and meaning beyond your performance is crucial. A strong spiritual connection provides a sense of purpose that transcends wins and losses, successes and failures. It offers a broader perspective, helping individuals maintain balance and resilience in the face of adversity.

Remember the mantra I wear under my baseball cap: G.F.E.B. - God, Family, Education, Baseball. This order of priorities has transformed my life and career, providing balance, purpose, and unshakeable confidence. It serves as a constant reminder that while excellence in our chosen field is important, it's not the sole defining factor of our worth or success.

As you embark on your journey to excellence, remember that true success demands more than just physical prowess or technical skill. It requires a harmonious blend of body, mind, and spirit. Embrace these principles, and you'll not only excel in your chosen field but also find fulfillment and purpose in every aspect of your life.

Are you ready to take your performance to the next level? The path to greatness awaits - it's time to step up to the plate and swing for the fences! Remember, excellence is not a destination, but a continuous journey of growth, learning, and self-discovery. By cultivating these five elements - skills, mental strength, knowledge, desire, and spiritual connection - you'll be well-equipped to face any challenge and achieve remarkable success in sports, business, and life.

Chapter Work Up

Skills and Fundamentals:

- What are your standout strengths in your sport or profession? Reflect deeply on your unique abilities and experiences that set you apart. Consider how these strengths can be leveraged to propel you towards excellence and leadership in your field.
- What areas of improvement have you identified in your sport or profession? Be honest and introspective. Recognizing these opportunities for growth is the first step towards mastering your craft and achieving your full potential.
- How can you transform your weaknesses into strengths? Develop a strategic action plan to address each area of improvement. Remember, every challenge overcome is a

step towards becoming an exceptional leader in sports, business, and life.

Competitive Psychology / Mental Training:

- Envision and articulate one compelling long-term goal that embodies your ultimate success:
- Dream big and be specific. This goal should inspire and drive you, serving as the north star for all your efforts.
- Identify two pivotal short-term goals that will pave the way to your long-term vision:
  - These should be challenging yet achievable milestones that build momentum and confidence.
  - Ensure these goals are specific, measurable, and time-bound to keep you focused and accountable.
- What are your primary stressors in your job or sport? Pinpoint these challenges and view them as opportunities for growth and resilience-building.
- How does stress manifest in your body? Understanding your physical stress responses is crucial for effective management and peak performance.
- What are your most effective strategies for managing stress and overcoming adversity? Develop a toolkit of techniques that work for you, enhancing your mental toughness and adaptability.

Knowledge of your sport or profession:

- Assess your current expertise in your profession or sport. How can you leverage this knowledge to stand out and make a significant impact?
- What have been your primary sources of information and learning in your field? Identify the most valuable resources that have shaped your expertise.
- How can you elevate your knowledge to the next level? Consider innovative learning strategies, mentorship opportunities, or cutting-edge research in your field.

Desire:

- What aspects of your job or sport ignite your passion? Harness these elements to fuel your motivation and drive for excellence.
- Which elements of your job or sport do you find challenging? How can you reframe these challenges as opportunities for growth and innovation?
- Imagine being forced to leave your current job or sport. How would this impact you, and why? This reflection can reveal the depth of your commitment and help you reconnect with your core motivations.
- What would inspire you to push beyond your current limits in your job or sport? Identify the key motivators that could unlock your next level of performance and leadership.

PERFORMANCE JOURNAL

Chapter 15
30-Day Mind and Body Challenge: Unlock Your Full Potential

Your mind is the epicenter of your energy, and breath is the vital bridge connecting your life to your conscious mind, uniting body and thought in a harmonious rhythm. But what if your thoughts are scattered, hindering you from finding this essential rhythm? This chapter is your key to unlocking the power within you.

If you've been following the Mental Master Training series, you know the truth: your mind holds all the answers. Your mission now is to harness a medium that concentrates your mind's dispersed energy into a laser-focused beam of potential. Are you ready to discover what that medium is?

St. Augustine, drawing from biblical wisdom, reminds us that the mind is created in God's image. Your mind inherently knows itself, always present and self-aware. However, in a world saturated with sensory distractions, it's easy to lose sight of your mind's true nature and potential. Too often, we attach ourselves to fleeting pleasures, resulting in materialistic pursuits that leave us unfulfilled.

This chapter is your gateway to profound self-knowledge. By following the meticulously crafted steps outlined here, you'll witness a remarkable growth in your self-awareness. Whether you're battling complacency, seeking motivation to break through perceived limits, or feeling like you've hit rock bottom, this 30-Day Reset Challenge is your lifeline. It's designed to transform you from the inside out, elevating your entire being and boosting your productivity in every aspect of life.

Are you prepared to embark on this life-changing journey? Let's dive into the first crucial step:

Step 1: Ignite Your Day with Positivity

Remember the Lord's promise in John 14:27 (ESV): "Peace I leave with you; my peace I give to you. Not as the world gives do I give to you. Let not your hearts be troubled, neither let them be afraid." Start each morning by immersing yourself in spiritual wisdom, whether it's a Bible verse or a devotional of your choice. Don't rush this sacred moment - it's your foundation for the day ahead.

What are you truly striving for? Happiness. But what is happiness if not the attainment of peace? Train your mind to recognize happiness in terms of inner peace and self-knowledge. Embrace the knowledge that a higher power is with you, urging you towards excellence in all your endeavors. If you're an athlete, let your ethics guide you to pursue your vocation with a pure heart.

The Challenging Road to Success

After all, virtue is "love that knows its priorities." So, ask yourself: have you truly prioritized your needs?

Step 2: Supercharge Your Success with Daily Goal Reviews

Self-assessment is your secret weapon for personal growth. It's a moment of reflection that illuminates your strengths and weaknesses, providing invaluable insights into your progress. By reviewing your goals daily, you open yourself up to tremendous opportunities for improvement and gain a clearer perspective on your development in relation to your peers.

What's your priority right now? Let's say it's perfecting your swing. You've been practicing relentlessly, and you're starting to see consistent, solid hits during training. This is your short-term, measurable goal. But what about your long-term vision? Perhaps it's hitting 10 home runs in the upcoming season. Remember, your long-term goals are the culmination of your short-term achievements. Start with attainable objectives - they're the stepping stones that will propel you towards your dreams with an unstoppable positive mindset.

Step 3: Fuel Your Body with a Powerful, Healthy Meal Plan

A healthy body is just as crucial as a healthy mind for living a fulfilling life. Embracing nutritious eating habits isn't just about maintaining a healthy weight or boosting your immune system - it's about transforming your entire well-being. A proper diet will shield you from life-threatening diseases like diabetes, cardiovascular issues, and high blood pressure, while simultaneously enhancing your efficiency, confidence, and emotional stability.

For athletes, a carefully crafted meal plan is non-negotiable. As a baseball coach, I can attest that this fast-paced, intensive sport demands a unique blend of motor skills, coordination, agility, speed, and strength. Baseball players need an optimal power-to-weight ratio to be both lightning-quick and formidably strong.

Commit to your meal plan with unwavering dedication. Remember, timing is crucial - disciplined eating enhances nutrient absorption, manages appetite, and maximizes fueling, recovery, training, and performance. Your body is your most valuable asset - treat it accordingly!

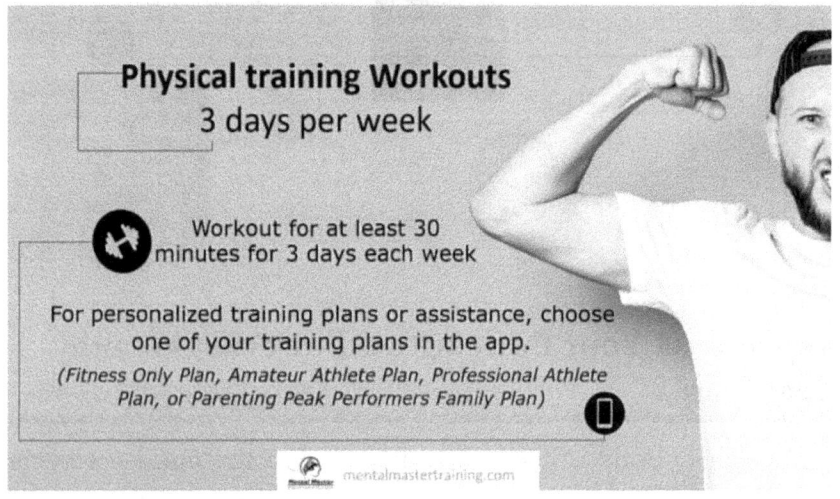

Step 4: Sculpt Your Body and Mind with Physical Training

Now that you've optimized your nutrition, it's time to focus on physical training. Commit to at least three intense training sessions per week for the next month. This isn't just for athletes - everyone should cultivate this habit for a healthier heart, better posture, and improved balance. Don't let the specter of future arthritis pain haunt you - take action now!

Athletes, your gym sessions are your secret weapon. They're not just about increasing agility and strength - they're about protecting your muscle mass, fortifying your bone health, and enhancing your body mechanics. Research shows that the neurochemical and neuromuscular responses to such exercises have profound positive effects on your brain, boosting your mood and skyrocketing your confidence.

Step 5: Supercharge Your Cardiovascular Health

There's no excuse to skip cardio - your body craves it! Whether it's running, biking, or rowing, find an aerobic exercise that resonates with you and commit to it three times a week. Need motivation? Let's delve into the incredible physiology behind it.

The Challenging Road to Success

During aerobic activity, you're engaging large muscle groups in your arms, legs, and hips. You'll notice immediate changes: faster, deeper breathing maximizing oxygen in your blood; accelerated heartbeat increasing blood flow to your muscles and lungs; widened capillaries delivering more oxygen to your muscles and flushing out waste products. Best of all, your body releases endorphins - natural painkillers that elevate your sense of well-being.

Athletes, cardio isn't just beneficial - it's as essential as breathing in your sporting life. It's time to embrace it with open arms!

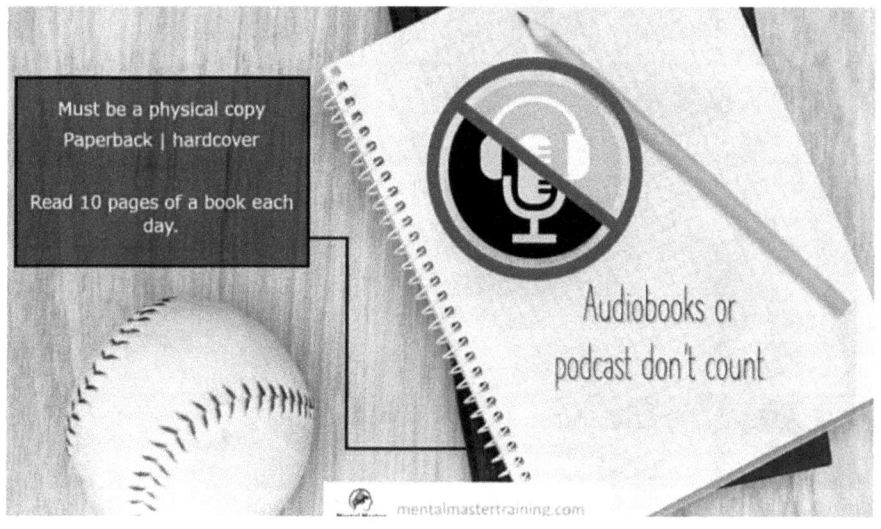

Step 6: Expand Your Mind with Daily Reading

In our digital age, where smartphones and social media constantly vie for our attention, it's crucial to reclaim your focus through reading physical books. Commit to reading at least 10 pages daily - it's a small step that yields enormous benefits.

Studies show that print readers score higher on empathy scales, likely due to the tactile sensation of holding a book. Feeling your progress through the pages creates a deeper connection with the story. More importantly, this daily reading habit cultivates consistency - a skill that will benefit every aspect of your life. Each day, you'll finish with a sense of accomplishment. Now, what will you do with all this positivity? It's time to spread it!

Step 7: Transform Lives with Daily Compliments

Complimenting others is a mark of true awareness and consciousness. It shows you've taken notice of someone's efforts, and trust me, people remember and value these acknowledgments. This simple act creates a positive ripple effect, enhancing social cohesion and mutual understanding.

Think of complimenting as a form of cognitive training - it sharpens your attention and amplifies positivity. The effects don't just benefit others; they bounce back to you, creating a more rewarding atmosphere for everyone. Science backs this up: praise activates the brain's reward centers, making it an incredibly effective motivator.

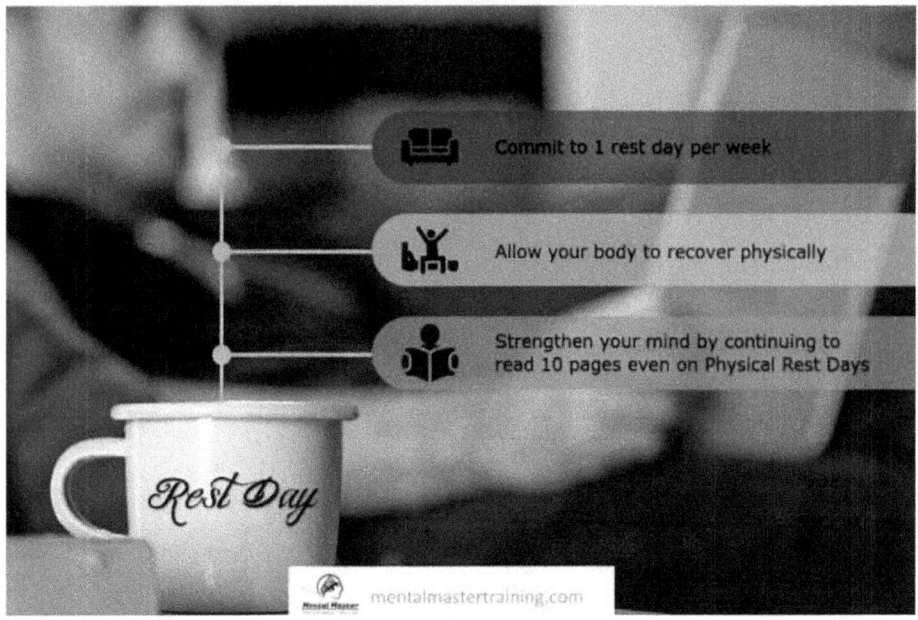

Step 8: Recharge Your Spirit with Weekly Rest

Rest isn't just important - it's essential. Researchers at Washington State University describe "waking rest" as the crucial fourth piece in the wellness puzzle, alongside exercise, nutrition, and sleep. It's your opportunity to reflect and connect with the deeper recesses of your mind.

For your body, rest is the secret ingredient to improvement. It allows your muscles to recover and rebuild, recharging you for the challenges ahead. Have you truly recharged yourself fully? There's still one missing piece in your daily routine. What could it be?

Step 9: Unlock Inner Peace with Daily Meditation

Meditation is your key to becoming fully alive in each moment. It's the thread that connects your body to your mind's consciousness, making you fully present in your waking life. This practice will strengthen your mind through the simple act of mindful breathing.

As you breathe in, maintain awareness of your breath without forcing it. Notice how this simple act brings your mind into harmony with your body. What's next on this transformative journey?

Step 10: Chronicle Your Growth with Daily Journaling

Skeptics might dismiss journaling, but its benefits are undeniable. At its core, journaling mirrors your progression. It's an exploration of language that equips you to better understand yourself and communicate with others. Your expanding vocabulary, courtesy of daily journaling, becomes a powerful tool in all aspects of life.

Journaling helps you connect with the present moment, setting aside future frustrations. It's intrinsically linked to mindfulness, bringing your wandering mind to attention and transforming your goals from passive wishes to active pursuits. The simple act of putting thoughts into words makes them tangible and achievable.

Through journaling, you untangle your mind and clarify your ambitions. Remember, while it demands self-discipline, the rewards are immeasurable.

Step 11: Rejuvenate Your Body and Mind with Quality Sleep

The final, crucial step in your transformation is ensuring you get at least 8 hours of sleep each night. Recent studies have revealed that during sleep, your brain flushes out waste material, including proteins linked to Alzheimer's disease. Adequate sleep is your shield against health issues and your ticket to feeling revitalized.

The National Sleep Foundation recommends 7-9 hours of sleep for adults aged 18-64, with children needing even more. Alarmingly, nearly 50% of people sleep less than the recommended average, leading to worse health outcomes including increased obesity, diabetes risk, and shorter lifespans.

Start your day on a positive note, expressing gratitude for life's blessings, and end it with restorative sleep. In between, live mindfully and purposefully. This chapter is your roadmap to a fulfilling, contented life.

Embrace this 30-Day Reset Challenge with unwavering commitment. Share this transformative journey with friends and family who need a boost in motivation and consistency. Together, we can create a ripple effect of positive change!

Thank you for allowing me to be part of your challenging yet rewarding road to success. For more insights, explore the Mental Master Training chapter series, where we'll continue to expand your knowledge and nurture your Mind, Body, and Soul. For personalized Mental Master Training Plans or Stress Management assistance, download the free Mental Master Performance App from your app store or visit mentalmastertraining.com. Until we meet again, may your days be blessed and your efforts unwavering. Your journey to greatness starts now!

Embark on a transformative 30-day journey towards success with our powerful checklist. This carefully crafted tool is designed to propel you forward, keeping you focused and motivated every step of the way. By leveraging the insights and strategies within, you'll not only track your progress but also unlock your full potential as a leader in sports, business, and life.

Don't just dream of success - actively pursue it. Our checklist serves as your personal roadmap, guiding you through each crucial step. As you tick off each accomplishment, you'll feel the momentum building, driving you closer to your goals. This is more than just a list; it's your partner in achievement, your catalyst for growth, and your blueprint for excellence.

Are you ready to revolutionize your approach and elevate your leadership skills? Seize this opportunity to transform your aspirations into reality. Your journey to becoming an influential Christian leader starts now. Embrace the challenge, commit to the process, and watch as you surpass your own expectations. Your success story begins with this checklist - let's make it extraordinary.

30-Day Mind and Body Challenge: Unlock Your Full Potential

30 Day Challenge Checklist

Day #____   Date:_____

__ Devotional

__ Review Goals

__ Healthy Meals

__ Workout

__ Cardio

__ Rest Day

__ 10 Pages

__ 2 compliments

__ Meditation

__ Reflect / Journal

__ 8 Hours Sleep

The Challenging Road to Success

30 Day Challenge Checklist

Day #_____   Date:_____

__ Devotional

__ Review Goals

__ Healthy Meals

__ Workout

__ Cardio

__ Rest Day

__ 10 Pages

__ 2 compliments

__ Meditation

__ Reflect / Journal

__ 8 Hours Sleep

30-Day Mind and Body Challenge: Unlock Your Full Potential

30 Day Challenge Checklist

Day #_____   Date:_____

__ Devotional

__ Review Goals

__ Healthy Meals

__ Workout

__ Cardio

__ Rest Day

__ 10 Pages

__ 2 compliments

__ Meditation

__ Reflect / Journal

__ 8 Hours Sleep

The Challenging Road to Success

30 Day Challenge Checklist

Day #_____   Date:_____

__ Devotional

__ Review Goals

__ Healthy Meals

__ Workout

__ Cardio

__ Rest Day

__ 10 Pages

__ 2 compliments

__ Meditation

__ Reflect / Journal

__ 8 Hours Sleep

30 Day Challenge Checklist

Day #_____   Date:_____

___ Devotional

___ Review Goals

___ Healthy Meals

___ Workout

___ Cardio

___ Rest Day

___ 10 Pages

___ 2 compliments

___ Meditation

___ Reflect / Journal

___ 8 Hours Sleep

The Challenging Road to Success

30 Day Challenge Checklist

Day #_____   Date:_____

__ Devotional

__ Review Goals

__ Healthy Meals

__ Workout

__ Cardio

__ Rest Day

__ 10 Pages

__ 2 compliments

__ Meditation

__ Reflect / Journal

__ 8 Hours Sleep

30-Day Mind and Body Challenge: Unlock Your Full Potential

30 Day Challenge Checklist

Day #____   Date:_____

___ Devotional

___ Review Goals

___ Healthy Meals

___ Workout

___ Cardio

___ Rest Day

___ 10 Pages

___ 2 compliments

___ Meditation

___ Reflect / Journal

___ 8 Hours Sleep

The Challenging Road to Success

30 Day Challenge Checklist

Day #_____   Date:_____

__ Devotional

__ Review Goals

__ Healthy Meals

__ Workout

__ Cardio

__ Rest Day

__ 10 Pages

__ 2 compliments

__ Meditation

__ Reflect / Journal

__ 8 Hours Sleep

30-Day Mind and Body Challenge: Unlock Your Full Potential

30 Day Challenge Checklist

Day #_____   Date:_____

__ Devotional

__ Review Goals

__ Healthy Meals

__ Workout

__ Cardio

__ Rest Day

__ 10 Pages

__ 2 compliments

__ Meditation

__ Reflect / Journal

__ 8 Hours Sleep

The Challenging Road to Success

30 Day Challenge Checklist

Day #_____   Date:_____

___ Devotional

___ Review Goals

___ Healthy Meals

___ Workout

___ Cardio

___ Rest Day

___ 10 Pages

___ 2 compliments

___ Meditation

___ Reflect / Journal

___ 8 Hours Sleep

30-Day Mind and Body Challenge: Unlock Your Full Potential

30 Day Challenge Checklist

Day # ____   Date: _____

__ Devotional

__ Review Goals

__ Healthy Meals

__ Workout

__ Cardio

__ Rest Day

__ 10 Pages

__ 2 compliments

__ Meditation

__ Reflect / Journal

__ 8 Hours Sleep

The Challenging Road to Success

30 Day Challenge Checklist

Day #_____   Date:_____

___ Devotional

___ Review Goals

___ Healthy Meals

___ Workout

___ Cardio

___ Rest Day

___ 10 Pages

___ 2 compliments

___ Meditation

___ Reflect / Journal

___ 8 Hours Sleep

30-Day Mind and Body Challenge: Unlock Your Full Potential

30 Day Challenge Checklist

Day #_____   Date:_____

__ Devotional

__ Review Goals

__ Healthy Meals

__ Workout

__ Cardio

__ Rest Day

__ 10 Pages

__ 2 compliments

__ Meditation

__ Reflect / Journal

__ 8 Hours Sleep

The Challenging Road to Success

30 Day Challenge Checklist

Day #_____   Date:_____

___ Devotional

___ Review Goals

___ Healthy Meals

___ Workout

___ Cardio

___ Rest Day

___ 10 Pages

___ 2 compliments

___ Meditation

___ Reflect / Journal

___ 8 Hours Sleep

30-Day Mind and Body Challenge: Unlock Your Full Potential

30 Day Challenge Checklist

Day #____   Date:_____

__ Devotional

__ Review Goals

__ Healthy Meals

__ Workout

__ Cardio

__ Rest Day

__ 10 Pages

__ 2 compliments

__ Meditation

__ Reflect / Journal

__ 8 Hours Sleep

The Challenging Road to Success

30 Day Challenge Checklist

Day #_____   Date:_____

__ Devotional

__ Review Goals

__ Healthy Meals

__ Workout

__ Cardio

__ Rest Day

__ 10 Pages

__ 2 compliments

__ Meditation

__ Reflect / Journal

__ 8 Hours Sleep

30-Day Mind and Body Challenge: Unlock Your Full Potential

30 Day Challenge Checklist

Day #____   Date:_____

__ Devotional

__ Review Goals

__ Healthy Meals

__ Workout

__ Cardio

__ Rest Day

__ 10 Pages

__ 2 compliments

__ Meditation

__ Reflect / Journal

__ 8 Hours Sleep

The Challenging Road to Success

30 Day Challenge Checklist

Day #_____   Date:_____

___ Devotional

___ Review Goals

___ Healthy Meals

___ Workout

___ Cardio

___ Rest Day

___ 10 Pages

___ 2 compliments

___ Meditation

___ Reflect / Journal

___ 8 Hours Sleep

30-Day Mind and Body Challenge: Unlock Your Full Potential

30 Day Challenge Checklist

Day #____   Date:_____

__ Devotional

__ Review Goals

__ Healthy Meals

__ Workout

__ Cardio

__ Rest Day

__ 10 Pages

__ 2 compliments

__ Meditation

__ Reflect / Journal

__ 8 Hours Sleep

The Challenging Road to Success

30 Day Challenge Checklist

Day #_____   Date:_____

___ Devotional

___ Review Goals

___ Healthy Meals

___ Workout

___ Cardio

___ Rest Day

___ 10 Pages

___ 2 compliments

___ Meditation

___ Reflect / Journal

___ 8 Hours Sleep

30-Day Mind and Body Challenge: Unlock Your Full Potential

30 Day Challenge Checklist

Day #____   Date:_____

__ Devotional

__ Review Goals

__ Healthy Meals

__ Workout

__ Cardio

__ Rest Day

__ 10 Pages

__ 2 compliments

__ Meditation

__ Reflect / Journal

__ 8 Hours Sleep

The Challenging Road to Success

30 Day Challenge Checklist

Day #_____   Date:_____

__ Devotional

__ Review Goals

__ Healthy Meals

__ Workout

__ Cardio

__ Rest Day

__ 10 Pages

__ 2 compliments

__ Meditation

__ Reflect / Journal

__ 8 Hours Sleep

30-Day Mind and Body Challenge: Unlock Your Full Potential

30 Day Challenge Checklist

Day #_____   Date:_____

___ Devotional

___ Review Goals

___ Healthy Meals

___ Workout

___ Cardio

___ Rest Day

___ 10 Pages

___ 2 compliments

___ Meditation

___ Reflect / Journal

___ 8 Hours Sleep

The Challenging Road to Success

30 Day Challenge Checklist

Day #_____   Date:_____

___ Devotional

___ Review Goals

___ Healthy Meals

___ Workout

___ Cardio

___ Rest Day

___ 10 Pages

___ 2 compliments

___ Meditation

___ Reflect / Journal

___ 8 Hours Sleep

30-Day Mind and Body Challenge: Unlock Your Full Potential

30 Day Challenge Checklist

Day #_____   Date:_____

__ Devotional

__ Review Goals

__ Healthy Meals

__ Workout

__ Cardio

__ Rest Day

__ 10 Pages

__ 2 compliments

__ Meditation

__ Reflect / Journal

__ 8 Hours Sleep

The Challenging Road to Success

30 Day Challenge Checklist

Day #_____   Date:_____

___ Devotional

___ Review Goals

___ Healthy Meals

___ Workout

___ Cardio

___ Rest Day

___ 10 Pages

___ 2 compliments

___ Meditation

___ Reflect / Journal

___ 8 Hours Sleep

30-Day Mind and Body Challenge: Unlock Your Full Potential

30 Day Challenge Checklist

Day #____   Date:_____

__ Devotional

__ Review Goals

__ Healthy Meals

__ Workout

__ Cardio

__ Rest Day

__ 10 Pages

__ 2 compliments

__ Meditation

__ Reflect / Journal

__ 8 Hours Sleep

The Challenging Road to Success

30 Day Challenge Checklist

Day #_____   Date:_____

__ Devotional

__ Review Goals

__ Healthy Meals

__ Workout

__ Cardio

__ Rest Day

__ 10 Pages

__ 2 compliments

__ Meditation

__ Reflect / Journal

__ 8 Hours Sleep

30-Day Mind and Body Challenge: Unlock Your Full Potential

30 Day Challenge Checklist

Day #____   Date:_____

__ Devotional

__ Review Goals

__ Healthy Meals

__ Workout

__ Cardio

__ Rest Day

__ 10 Pages

__ 2 compliments

__ Meditation

__ Reflect / Journal

__ 8 Hours Sleep

The Challenging Road to Success

30 Day Challenge Checklist

Day #_____   Date:_____

___ Devotional

___ Review Goals

___ Healthy Meals

___ Workout

___ Cardio

___ Rest Day

___ 10 Pages

___ 2 compliments

___ Meditation

___ Reflect / Journal

___ 8 Hours Sleep

A Heartfelt Thank You

Your decision to invest time in reading this book means the world to me. As my third published work, it represents a significant milestone in my mission to empower individuals like you to excel in sports, business, and life. My deepest hope is that these pages will ignite a spark within you, propelling you towards unprecedented success, improved health, or a renewed connection with God.

Your journey with this book doesn't have to end here. I invite you to share your thoughts and experiences through a review on Amazon, Barnes & Noble, or your preferred book platform. Your honest feedback is invaluable - it not only helps other readers make informed decisions but also guides me in refining my craft for future works.

As a token of my appreciation for your support, I encourage you to explore my previous publications and stay tuned for upcoming releases. Visit www.davidangeron.com to discover more resources designed to fuel your personal and professional growth. Together, let's continue this inspiring journey towards leadership and success in all aspects of life.

www.ingramcontent.com/pod-product-compliance
Lightning Source LLC
Chambersburg PA
CBHW071329190426
43193CB00041B/1033